Welsh History and its S

Post-War Wales

Post-War Wales

Edited by

Trevor Herbert
Gareth Elwyn Jones

Cardiff
University of Wales Press
1995

University of Wales Press, 6 Gwennyth Street, Cathays, Cardiff CF2 4YD

A catalogue record for this book is available from the British Library.

ISBN 0-7083-1291-8

Cover Design : Cloud Nine Design
The publishers wish to acknowledge the advice and assistance given by the Design Department of the Welsh Books Council.

Typeset at University of Wales Press

Printed in Wales by Gwasg Dinefwr, Llandybïe

Contents

Illustrations

Acknowledgements

Our greatest debt is to the contributors who helpfully kept to the prescribed format for the series and the tight schedules we imposed on them. Dr W.D. Jones of University of Wales, Cardiff, did most of the work preparing photographic and other illustrations for the book and we count ourselves lucky to have had his expertise available to us. We are grateful also to Annette Musker for her meticulous preparation of the index.

Julia Carey keyed in and compiled the handover disk and manuscript from a variety of diverse formats and she also pointed out a number of infelicities in the earliest drafts of the manuscript. A number of colleagues at the Open University in Wales were extremely helpful but Kath Williams, and, latterly, Nia Jones, were the most directly involved in the project.

We are particularly grateful to Ruth Dennis-Jones our copy-editor at the University of Wales Press. Her critical reading of the manuscript led her to suggest a number of important points which improved the book considerably. If any shortcomings remain they can be laid firmly at our door.

TREVOR HERBERT
GARETH ELWYN JONES
Cardiff
1995

The Contributors

JANET DAVIES is a free-lance researcher and writer.

CHRISTOPHER HARVIE is Professor of British Studies at the University of Tübingen.

TREVOR HERBERT is Senior Lecturer in Music, and Arts Staff Tutor at the Open University in Wales. He specializes in British music history.

ROB HUMPHREYS is Lecturer in Cultural Studies in the Department of Adult and Continuing Education at the University of Wales, Swansea.

GARETH ELWYN JONES is Research Professor of Education at the University of Wales, Aberystwyth.

KENNETH O. MORGAN is Principal of the University of Wales, Aberystwyth, and Vice-Chancellor of the University of Wales.

TERESA REES is Reader in Labour Market Studies at the School for Advanced Urban Studies, University of Bristol.

PETER STEAD is Senior Lecturer in History at the University of Wales, Swansea.

Preface

This is the seventh volume to be published in the Welsh History and its Sources series. The previous volumes were prepared under the auspices of a Welsh Office research and development grant. The grant was given to promote and facilitate the study of Welsh history among adult learners and, particularly, to embody the principles implied in terms such as 'open learning' and 'distance learning'. The former suggests the need for volumes to be accessible and free-standing so that readers are not assumed to have followed a prerequisite programme of study in order to benefit from them. The latter suggests a pedagogical technique or method that does not rely on teachers: students should be able to benefit from the material without additional support.

These intentions, however laudable, often came close to being in conflict with our other, perhaps more earnest, ambition for the volumes: that they should be immediately recognizable as books rather than as 'educational materials'. In other words, we were keen that the individual titles in the series should contain engaging and new discourse on Welsh history. It is a cause of satisfaction to us that previous books in the series have been widely distributed and have become commonly used texts in schools and universities as well as being popular with more general readers.

The basic format for each volume is always the same. Authors are commissioned to write essays on topics that fall within their area of expertise. Annexed to each essay is a collection of sources linked explicitly and obviously to the essay. This system offers at least two directions from which the material can be approached. Each section is, in its own right, an illustrated discourse on a topic of Welsh history. Also, each is a collection of sources with an example of how one writer has used and interpreted them.

This is not a history of Wales during the period 1945 to 1990, certainly not a comprehensive history. Rather it is a series of examples of how writers have interpreted some themes and topics that have emerged as interesting or important during that period. The choice of topics was difficult. With the events of this period being so vivid in the memories of the editors the process of agreeing omissions was tortuous. We are confident that the balance of the book is right but there are obvious omissions caused by the limitations of space. It would have been good to have looked at change in religion in Wales since the war. Also, we thought long and hard before deciding not to include a discrete section on the media. A glaring omission is in the area of change in education in Wales. Gareth Elwyn Jones's introductory essay, in concentrating on educational development in Wales since the war is, in part, a compensation for this omission but we also felt it appropriate that education, the single most common and shared experience for those experiencing childhood or parenthood in Wales in the post-war years, provided a microcosm of so many of the important issues which have stimulated debate in post-war Wales.

Timechart

Wales		Other significant events
	1942	Publication of the Beveridge Report.
	1944	Education Act (R.A. Butler).
	1945	End of the Second World War. General election; first overall majority for a Labour government.
Welsh National Opera established.	**1946**	
	1947	Nationalization of the coal-mines, railways and electricity.
Glamorgan win the county cricket championship. Creation of Council for Wales and Monmouthshire.	**1948**	National Insurance and National Health Service begin.
Welsh Joint Education Committee established	**1949**	
Welsh rugby team win the Grand Slam.	**1950**	General election; Labour re-elected.

Minister for Welsh Affairs appointed. Port Talbot steelworks opened.	**1951**	General election; Conservatives win.
Welsh rugby team win Grand Slam. Cardiff City A.F.C. win promotion to the First Division.	**1952**	
Broadcasting Council for Wales established. First broadcast of a Welsh-language television programme. Welsh rugby team beat the New Zealand All Blacks.	**1953**	
Under Milk Wood first broadcast.	**1954**	
Cardiff declared capital of Wales.	**1955**	General election; Conservatives re-elected.
Ysgol Glan Clwyd, the first bilingual secondary school, opens in Flintshire.	**1956**	
Act passed allowing the drowning of Tryweryn. Bill Haley and the Comets appear in Cardiff.	**1957**	
Commercial television by TWW (Television Wales and the West) starts transmissions in Wales.	**1958**	

	1959	General election; Conservatives re-elected.
Death of Aneurin Bevan. *Welsh History Review* starts publication.	1960	
Welsh Books Council set up.	1961	
Tynged yr Iaith broadcast by Saunders Lewis. Cymdeithas yr Iaith Gymraeg founded. Llanwern steelworks opened.	1962	
Hughes Parry Committee on status of the Welsh language.	1963	
Welsh rugby team win Triple Crown seven times.	1964–79	
BBC Wales established. James Griffiths appointed first secretary of state for Wales. Glamorgan's first victory over the Australian cricket team.	1964	General election; Labour government elected.
Poetry Wales starts publication	1965	Circular 10/65 – required local authorities to draw up plans for comprehensive schools.
Aberfan disaster. Cledwyn Hughes becomes secretary of state for Wales. Gwynfor Evans, Plaid Cymru, wins parliamentary seat in Carmarthen. Severn Bridge opened.	1966	General election; Labour re-elected.

Welsh Language Act passed.   **1967**
Welsh Arts Council
established.

Harlech Television (HTV)   **1968**
takes over from TWW.
George Thomas becomes
secretary of state for Wales.

Glamorgan win county cricket   **1969**   Open University founded.
championship.
Investiture of Prince of Wales.

Peter Thomas becomes   **1970**   General election;
secretary of state for Wales.   Conservatives win.

Mudiad Ysgolion Meithrin   **1971**
(Welsh-language nursery
school movement) starts.
Planet first published.

Sports Council for Wales   **1972**   UK enters European
established.   Economic Community.

  1973   Kilbrandon Report on the
  constitution.

Eight county councils form   **1974**   General elections in February
the main tier of local   and October; both won by
government.   Labour.
  Local government
  reorganized.

  1975   Referendum confirms UK
  membership of EEC.

BBC Radio Wales and Radio   **1977**
Cymru first listed as separate
services.

Devolution referendum. Nicholas Edwards becomes secretary of state for Wales. Establishment of Parliamentary Select Committee for Welsh Affairs.	**1979**	Conservatives win general election.
Swansea City A.F.C. promoted to First Division.	**1981**	
Launch of Sianel Pedwar Cymru (S4C).	**1982**	Falklands War.
Neil Kinnock becomes leader of the Labour Party.	**1983**	General election; Conservatives re-elected.
	1984–5	Miners' strike.
Peter Walker becomes secretary of state for Wales. Honno, the Welsh women's press, founded.	**1987**	General election; Conservatives re-elected.
	1988	Education Reform Act establishes creation of a National Curriculum.
David Hunt becomes secretary of state for Wales. Last coal-mine in Rhondda Valley closes.	**1990**	
John Redwood becomes secretary of state for Wales.	**1992**	General election; Conservatives re-elected.

Welsh Language Act passed   **1993**
making the Welsh Language
Board statutory.
Publication of collected poems
of R.S. Thomas.

Welsh-language film *Hedd Wyn*   **1994**
nominated for an Oscar.

                                      1995–6 Local government reorganized
again.

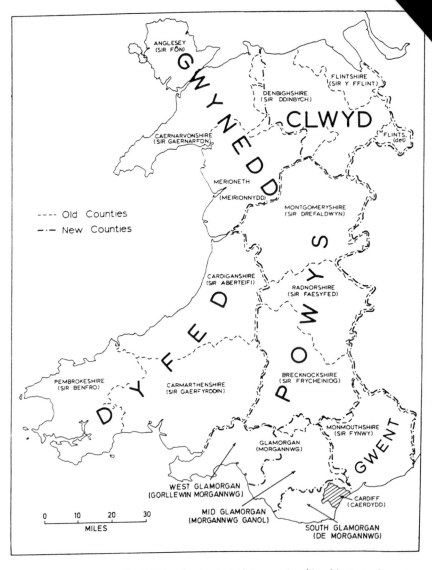

The main administrative units of Wales, showing the 'old' (pre-1974) and 'new' (1974–1996) county boundaries. (*Source: D. Huw Owen (ed.)*, Settlement and Society in Wales, *Cardiff, 1989.*)

Post-War Wales

GARETH ELWYN JONES

The purpose of this book is consistent with that of companion volumes in the series: to provide interpretations of the kaleidoscope of happenings over time (in this case the last half century), and some insights into the raw material on which those interpretations rest. However, it might be argued that the nature of the task is rather different in a volume which deals with contemporary Wales. While all historical writing reflects elements of the authors' personality, distance lends greater disinterest. When historians attempt to impose patterns on events in which they have themselves been participants — however passive — those patterns may be more subjective and more distorted than with earlier periods of history. The nature of the sources has been modified. For very recent history the historian is, to however marginal a degree, his or her own source, with some lines of enquiry, perhaps some factual information, emanating from personal experience. Particularly significant also is the technological revolution of the last fifty years. The cave drawings of Altamira or Lascaux, of course, pre-date the written word, but nothing has foreshadowed the impact of the visual images of the ubiquitous television pictures which dominate the leisure hours of all generations.

Yet it might be argued equally forcefully that the concerns of individuals, families and societies remain essentially the same. The transmission of those grainy monochrome newsreels of the D-Day landings with which the fiftieth anniversary was recalled evoke a seemingly distant world of outdated weaponry, transport and equipment. Yet there were few extended families in whom the same newsreels did not promote poignant memories. Those who survived unscathed in 1945 speak now, as they did then, of their determination at the time that no future generations would be subjected to similar experiences. There were many in Britain who were also determined that the war should see the end of the kind of society which had tolerated the Depression of the inter-war years, that the waste of life in wartime should not see a return to blighted lives in peacetime.

In this context the principles of the Beveridge Report, published in 1942, which were to form the basis of the welfare state, had a particular relevance to Wales because so much of the country had been devastated by the decline of heavy industry in the inter-war years. With a determination fostered by the common sacrifice of war that Britain should build a fairer post-war society, the Labour Party was swept into government in 1945. Welsh radicalism, once channelled so effectively into Liberalism, was now predominantly socialist and, as a result of the 1945 election, in the mainstream. Welsh MPs, particularly Aneurin Bevan, were now able to play their part in translating a social programme forged in the most adverse economic conditions into a welfare state. But that state was not Welsh. Bevan, in particular, would have no truck with the creation of specifically Welsh institutions. Indeed, in Wales as in the rest of Britain, the priorities of people and politicians in the aftermath of war were economic and social reconstruction.

The Labour governments of 1945–51 forged a new Britain, and Wales took its share of the benefits. A broad political consensus, encompassing the welfare state and high rates of employment, determined that the Conservative administrations which were in power for thirteen years after 1951 allowed the great majority in Wales, as elsewhere, to participate in growing economic prosperity, especially from about 1955. Gradually, motor cars, washing machines and television sets symbolized revolutions in patterns of work and leisure. Again, there was nothing peculiarly Welsh about these changes. On the contrary, such changes in transport and communication threatened traditional manifestations of Welshness. In some chapels in Wales the time of the evening service was rescheduled to allow congregations to watch episodes of the *Forsyte Saga* on television. More compelling was the realization after the 1951 census that the number of Welsh speakers had declined so substantially in the twenty years since the previous census. Reaction took many forms as a more affluent society could afford to extend its vision. The threat to the language, and to other manifestations of Welshness, were taken increasingly seriously and Janet Davies's chapter informs us of some of the responses. Kenneth O. Morgan's essay explains that political nationalism, of the most marginal significance immediately after the war, impinged increasingly on public consciousness in the 1960s.

No book dealing with the plethora of subjects and source material in this period can aim to be comprehensive. Some of the essays which follow concentrate substantially on events within Wales but we insure against introspection by including essays dealing with the relationship of Wales with Europe and a wider world, and with some of the images which Wales projects to that world. It must always remain that the complexity of the story even within Wales itself defies full analysis. Let us take just one example. Perhaps the only institutional experience which all readers of histories of Wales have in common is school. For better or worse we have, with the rarest of exceptions, been compelled by law to attend school from the age of five to the age of fourteen or more. It is all the more remarkable, therefore, that the history of schools in Wales often merits hardly a mention in general histories. One clue to the extent of consequent deficiencies in historical analysis is supplied by Peter Stead's essay on popular culture, which makes the intriguing point that one of the most significant social divides in post-war Wales was that between the products of the grammar schools and those who went to secondary modern schools (or even the all-age secondary schools which took an unconscionable time to phase out). Authors and editors never recognize such a divide in the historical patterns they impose by their chapter headings — as they do, for example, by commissioning separate chapters on women's history — yet its significance cannot be underrated. Indeed, the existence of a discriminatory examination for all pupils at the age of eleven, and its discontinuance with the coming of comprehensive schools, raises the most profound questions about the political, social and cultural history of Wales in the post-war period.

First, it reminds us of a theme basic to this book, the relationship between the historian and his or her sources. The editors and those authors who have written about the history of Wales in the chapters which follow attended schools which operated under an education system formulated by the Education Act of 1944. Those of us who were pupils in the Welsh grammar schools remember school uniforms, lessons in a strict hierarchy of subjects, O level examinations, a segregated sixth form for the élite, begowned masters and mistresses (rather than teachers) possessed of a dramatic variety of intimidatory weapons, Saturday morning games and an array of extra-curricular activities. This whole complex of pleasure or misery was made accessible by success in that dreaded, ubiquitous eleven-plus examination. So much was part of our day-to-day experience, branded on our personalities and ingrained on our memories. What we did not understand was that we were pawns in a game of political power and fodder for social experiment, and that our schooling experience was to affect the linguistic and cultural history of Wales.

Secondly, historians have stressed the success of the partnership between central and local government for more than three decades after the war. In fact the way in which the 1944 Education Act was implemented in Wales illustrates the tensions which have always existed between the localities and central administrations. They also have a Welsh dimension which illuminates the uneasy nature of the relationship between Wales and England in the post-war period.

Under the terms of the 1944 Act, local authorities had to submit plans for the reorganization of education in their areas. Counties and county boroughs in Wales were constrained in two directions. In the most rural areas, given physical distances and the scattered population, it did not make sense to establish separate grammar and secondary modern schools for pupils between the ages of eleven and fifteen. Therefore, often reluctantly, the rural local authorities established some bilateral schools, taking in all pupils from the local catchment area. One council, far less reluctantly, moved immediately towards the establishment of bilateral/multilateral schools and, by 1953, Anglesey became the first local authority in Wales or England to provide secondary education in area secondary schools rather than by selection at the age of eleven.

In two of the most populous parts of Wales a more overtly political problem presented itself. The education committees of Glamorgan County Council and Swansea County Borough Council submitted plans which proposed the creation of different kinds of multilateral area secondary schools. These plans arose out of a belief in the ideal of equality of opportunity and the injustice of a segregating examination at the age of eleven, rather than of any geographical necessity. As such, they were unacceptable to senior civil servants in the Ministry of Education and its Welsh Department who successfully directed their political masters into establishing a system of bipartite/tripartite education. This was based on a rigid distinction between the more academic pupils who proceeded to grammar schools, having passed the eleven-plus, and those of a more 'concrete' cast of mind (to cite the Norwood Report of 1943) whose secondary education took place in secondary modern schools. In this way the future life chances of the population were determined at the age of eleven, because Ministry officials also ensured that external examinations, which provided entrance to university and teacher-training college for the select few, should be restricted to grammar-school pupils who completed a course terminating beyond the statutory leaving age. While civil servants reluctantly allowed geographical factors to determine breaches in the grammar/secondary modern system in some areas of rural Wales, they were implacably opposed to any infringement on doctrinal grounds. Neither Swansea nor Glamorgan got its multilateral schools. The grammar/secondary modern divide was almost universally applied in both areas, with the result noted by Peter Stead. The Ministry allowed only two multilateral schools in Swansea — Penlan and Mynydd-bach — on the grounds that they were 'experimental'. But there was more to it. These schools were tolerated because they served new working-class housing estates. Post-war educational structures and civil servants' class judgements went hand in hand. The outcome of the 1944 Education Act in Wales indicates that, in the last resort, the partnership between central government and local authorities was extremely unequal.

Despite Secretary of State Anthony Crosland's Circular 10/65 of 1965, which impelled local authorities towards reorganization along comprehensive-school lines, central government's grip on the administration of education and, especially, curriculum, loosened in the 1960s and 1970s. However, the Welsh experience indicates that there should be no surprise that in the 1970s (and Prime Minister Callaghan's Ruskin College speech of 1976 was the major public manifestation of it) central government's ministers and civil servants set out to reassert control. By means of the 1988 Education Act, the National Curriculum and an unceasing stream of legislation and administrative reordering, government dogma has pushed civil servants many a bridge further than they anticipated in the late 1970s.

Thirdly, decision-making in education provides a vivid example of a central paradox in post-war Wales: that there has been an increasing number of administrative bodies exclusive to Wales which have implemented policies neither emanating from Wales nor necessarily reflecting public opinion within Wales. Symbolically, there has been a significant Welsh dimension to post-war reorganization of schools. Although it resulted in ending an administratively separate set of Welsh secondary schools, first established under an Act of 1889 which applied only to Wales, there were still Welsh administrative structures in being. One

was the Central Welsh Board, largely made up of local authority represⁿ
entatives, which gave way in 1949 to the Welsh Joint Education
Committee. Aptly, perhaps, in view of the balance of power which had
been evident in the post-war settlement, the Welsh Department of the
Board of Education, established in 1907, had long ago asserted its
supremacy over the CWB. In turn, the Welsh Department of the new
Ministry of Education, situated in London, followed the policies of its
parent body in implementing a divided system of secondary schools.
Policies of central government were to be carried out as far as possible;
any adaptation to meet the peculiar needs of Wales was a departure
form the norm rather than a policy for Wales. Under the 1944
Education Act an Advisory Council for England was paralleled by an
Advisory Council (Wales). Both were nominated bodies. In 1947 the
Welsh Advisory Council advocated that all Welsh secondary schools
should be bilateral or multilateral. The Council's advice was totally
ignored.

Central-government control over the education system weakened in
the 1960s and early 1970s at a time when there were increasing devolutionary trends in educational administration. At first it was tokenism; in
1947 an office of the Welsh Department of the Ministry of Education
was established in Cardiff, the first time that any aspect of its work had
gone outside Whitehall. Then, five years later, most of the Welsh
Department's work was transferred to Cardiff. In 1963 the new perma-
nent secretary of the Department was based in Cardiff — for the first
time since the inception of the Department in 1907. By 1970 the implications for education of the creation of a secretaryship of state for
Wales six years previously became apparent. All responsibility for
primary and secondary education was transferred to the secretary of
state for Wales.

For the moment the implications of this were disguised by a consen-
sual approach to school organization and reorganization. In particular,
the movement towards 'comprehensivization', gathering pace in the
1970s, roused very little opposition in Wales (Cardiff was an exception).
But as soon as central government determined to claw back control of
the system at the expense of local authorities and teachers' unions, the
education situation in Wales illuminated the wider Welsh condition.

Since 1979, Conservative governments have been in power, while,
as Kenneth O. Morgan's essay reveals, commanding only a minority of
parliamentary seats in Wales. The policies of these governments,

especially since the mid-eighties, have been to centralize control of the curriculum and testing, and to devolve detailed administration, including finance, to individual schools. This strange mixture of centralization and decentralization has been necessary to allow the ultimate goal of competition and market forces to operate in the inimical world of education. In this situation the strains inherent in Welsh governmental structures have become particularly evident. Despite devolutionary devices, the secretary of state for Wales and the Welsh Office Education Department have implemented these policies, as happened in the 1940s and 1950s, without regard to their suitability in the Welsh situation. City technology colleges and specialist schools for particular subjects are of the most marginal relevance to Wales. Market forces may or may not be appropriate to urban Wales but they are a wholly inappropriate motor for change in rural Wales. The drive towards grant-maintained schools, independent of local authorities, has had singularly little response in Wales, affecting only sixteen schools so far, yet the individual grants being offered to them by the Welsh Office are vastly greater than for those remaining with the local authorities. Subsidiarity, it seems, is an ephemeral concept. Wales cannot be allowed to diverge. Has anything changed since the 1940s?

The degree of independence allowed to educational institutions in Wales therefore prompts a whole range of questions about the nature of the government of Wales as a whole. The minister of state in the Welsh Office takes responsibility for education in Wales under the overall charge of the secretary of state for Wales. A raft of educational quangos in England is replicated in Wales. There are Higher and Further Education Funding Councils for Wales and, in 1994, the Curriculum Council for Wales gave way to a Curriculum and Assessment Authority for Wales. The inspection of schools in Wales is organized by a separate inspectorate. Yet it remains that major policy initiatives have not been formulated with the needs of Wales in mind; the most that has been allowed is adaptation at the margin.

Fourthly, reorientation in the content of school education in Wales has raised essential questions about the nature of 'Welshness', to the extent that the former chief executive of the Schools Curriculum and Assessment Authority, charged with planning the curriculum for England, has used the example of Wales to argue for a similar debate about the nature of an English cultural heritage. Success indeed! At first glance this would seem to cast doubt on earlier concentration on the stark limitations of Welsh autonomy. In the immediate post-war years, subject matter in Welsh schools was governed substantially by tradition and the examination system. Secondary (grammar) school curricula had been laid down by regulation at the beginning of the century and, despite loosening of this control, the menu of academic subjects had been little modified. The hierarchy of subjects which had been maintained by matriculation requirements still dominated thinking — and requirements for university entrance which, from the 1950s, was regulated by Ordinary and Advanced level examinations. In the secondary modern — and indeed the all-age schools — the curriculum was far more utilitarian. Despite the transition to comprehensive schools and the raising of the school-leaving age the divide was maintained into the 1980s — until the advent of the General Certificate of Secondary Education — by the separate O level and CSE examinations. The latter were intended for the middle cohort in the ability range and were far more practical. Their currency was limited.

The external examination system was particularly significant since central government control over the curriculum was less marked than at any time in the history of state education. From 1964 the Schools Council, with its teacher majority, was entrusted with curricular initiatives which included a range of exciting subject projects but no attempt to tackle the problem of the whole curriculum. Although there was a Schools Council Committee for Wales it inevitably echoed the parent body's piecemeal approach. Therefore the one substantial overview of the 'Welshness' of the whole curriculum which it produced had little impact. As doubts about Britain's economic performance and the education and training practices which underpinned it escalated, so civil service and government pronouncements more overtly invaded the secret garden of the curriculum. James Callaghan's 1976 Ruskin College speech publicized the new agenda. Curriculum concerns meshed eventually with political dogma to produce the 1988 Education Act. This Act provided for a curriculum which was to be taught in all schools in England and Wales. The list of subjects was drawn up by Secretary of State Kenneth Baker personally and certainly without consultation with any Welsh interest. However, its form and implementation have had unforeseen consequences for Wales. A traditional subject-based curriculum encapsulated notions of education as the transmission of cultural heritage; the concept of a 'national' cultural heritage immediately raised questions as to which nation's heritage was involved. The issues were then fought out on intellectual and institutional bases. The ambitions of the Welsh Office Education Department and the Curriculum Council for Wales to stake out their independence meshed with theoretical analyses to produce a National Curriculum for Wales which is substantially at variance with that in England. The Welsh language, though not now to be compulsory as a second language beyond the age of fourteen, has a more secure place than ever before. The history and geography of Wales have merited different degrees of separate treatment, as have music and art.

The 'Welshness' which these differences represent is interesting. Historical and cultural differences in the Welsh experience are obviously reflected. But some distinctions in music and art reflect something more subtle — a significantly greater degree of teacher influence in Wales and its encouragement by the Curriculum Council for Wales. The limits to this, on the other hand, have been vividly demonstrated by the fate of the controversial curriculum in English. Welsh wishes for more teacher autonomy and less prescription of content, finding approval in the Curriculum Council for Wales, have not been allowed to shape the nature of this core subject in the schools of Wales. Wales has to follow England. Nothing more vividly encapsulates the nature of Welsh autonomy.

The education story since 1945 illuminates themes crucial to the Welsh experience: the nature of democracy in Wales, the relationship between central and local government, cultural distinctiveness — in both languages — and its transmission, the fate of the Welsh language in an era of population mobility, chameleon communities and mixed employment prospects. The recent history of education in Wales, like the other histories which follow, is ample indication that the matter of Wales in the 1990s requires a response from us all.

Wales since 1945: Political Society

KENNETH O. MORGAN

The political culture of Wales entered a decisive new phase with
the landslide Labour victory in the general election of July 1945.
Buoyed up by the mood of social solidarity generated by years
of war, fortified by bitter memories of the depression and
industrial stagnation, Labour achieved an even more sweeping
triumph in Wales than in Britain as a whole. It ended up with
twenty-five seats, including seven gains, and its share of the poll
(at 58.5 per cent) was over ten points higher than in Britain as a
whole. Everywhere there was a euphoric mood of social
change, and in the south Wales valleys some immense Labour
majorities. Cliff Prothero, organizer and secretary of the Welsh
regional council of Labour, refers to a remarkable event in
Abertillery where Labour's majority was over 24,000 but where
the Labour agent nevertheless called for a recount to try to
A.1   make certain that the Tory candidate had lost his deposit (A.1).
Against this, the demoralized Conservatives retained only four
seats, Monmouth in the anglicized south-east, Flintshire,
Denbighshire and Caernarfon Boroughs on the north Wales
coast. In Caernarfon Boroughs, an era came to an end, with
Lloyd George's old constituency falling to the Conservatives
shortly after the death of the veteran statesman, recently
elevated to the Lords. The Liberals clung on to seven, essentially rural, seats, with Lloyd George's daughter, Lady Megan,
retaining Anglesey, and his son, Gwilym (shortly to defect to
the Conservatives) hanging on to Pembrokeshire. Nearly all the
eight Plaid Cymru candidates lost their deposits.

For the next six years, Labour set the political agenda
for Wales as for Britain as a whole. Welsh politicians were

prominent in the party and the administration at all levels. Aneurin Bevan, as minister of health, introduced the great social landmark of the National Health Service. James Griffiths passed the National Insurance Act of 1946 and later was to become colonial secretary. Other prominent Welshmen in the government included Ness Edwards and Lord (George) Hall, while in Transport House, Morgan Phillips, the Welsh-speaking son of an Aberdare miner, was the supreme *apparatchik*. While there were criticisms of Ernest Bevin's cold-war foreign policy, in general Labour opinion in Wales remained extremely enthusiastic at the Attlee government's achievements, notably the launching of the welfare state, the sustaining of full employment, and the nationalizing of major industries and utilities. The nationalization of the coal-mines on 1 January 1947 was greeted with intense and passionate enthusiasm all over the south Wales coalfield — 'Today the mines belong to the people'.

In the election of 1950, when Labour's majority nationally slumped from over 150 to a mere six overall, the party's hold over Welsh political culture scarcely weakened. Labour held twenty-seven of the thirty-six Welsh seats (after redistribution), as against five for the Liberals and four for the Conservatives and allies. Even in the general election of October 1951, when Attlee was finally defeated, Labour still held on to twenty-seven seats, and its share of the poll, at over 60 per cent, was actually higher than in the halcyon year of 1945. Losses to the Conservatives in Conway in north Wales and Barry in the far south were balanced by Labour gains from the Liberals in the Welsh-speaking rural constituencies of Anglesey (where Lady Megan Lloyd George was defeated by Cledwyn Hughes) and Merioneth. There were signs that in north and mid Wales the advance of Labour had far from reached its natural limit.

During these years of post-war reconstruction, austerity and economic stringency, the main emphasis was on national planning. Labour's ethic was one of nation-wide solidarity and the united advance of the British working class. Demands heard in the 1945 general election for a secretary of state for Wales led nowhere. Welsh nationalism as a political force was in the doldrums, while Attlee, Morrison and other leading ministers set their face firmly against concessions to separatism. There

Leaflet advertising events to celebrate the nationalization of the coal industry in 1947. (*Source: Welsh Industrial and Maritime Museum.*)

A.2

were discussions within the government about the administration of Wales in the 1946–8 period (A.2). While Herbert Morrison placed the emphasis on nation-wide planning which would subsume Wales within the imperatives of the British economy, James Griffiths tried in vain to have Wales treated as a separate area within the nationalized electricity industry in December 1946 (as happened later with gas). The Cabinet's Machinery of Government Committee in 1948 rejected the idea of a Welsh secretary of state, with Aneurin Bevan particularly hostile. However, a concession was made in the creation of a Council for Wales as a purely advisory body, although Herbert Morrison refused to allow a Cabinet minister to serve as its chairman because of 'difficulties that might arise'. Despite the vigour of Huw T. Edwards, the trade unionist appointed as its first chairman, the Council for Wales remained a somewhat shadowy body. At the start of the period of Conservative government in 1951, Welsh politics appeared to be almost indistinguishable from those of the United Kingdom as a whole.

The politics of the fifties in Wales as elsewhere were dominated by the growth of affluence. Wages rose; unemployment virtually disappeared; Welsh people enjoyed the growing benefits of home ownership, car ownership and consumer-led market prosperity, along with such novelties as holidays abroad. Even rural Wales benefited from the growing affluence of the period since the Conservatives largely followed Labour's previous policy of using ministerial powers to assist agriculture and direct industry into Wales via the Board of Trade's regional policies. Advance factories were created to repair the loss of employment caused by the decay of older industries such as tin-plate and coal. In 1959–60, there was another surge of activity with the car industry entrenching itself in the Welsh economy, with the Rover works in Cardiff and the Fisher-Ludlow body-press works at Llanelli. In 1962 the giant RTB/Spencer steel plant opened at Llanwern near Newport to become, like the Steel Company of Wales, established at Port Talbot just after the war, one of the great steel-producing plants of Europe.

In their thirteen years of power, the Conservatives devoted a surprising amount of attention to Wales, considering their relative weakness in that part of Britain. In 1946, R.A. Butler had foreshadowed the Conservatives in creating some kind of minister as what he called 'an Ambassador for Wales' (A.3). In 1951 Sir David Maxwell-Fyfe, a Scot, became the first minister for Welsh affairs, being succeeded in 1954 by Gwilym Lloyd-George, now a hyphenated Conservative, who was also home secretary. In 1957 he was followed by the Englishman, Henry Brooke, minister for housing and local government; a somewhat maladroit choice by Macmillan, he was eventually replaced by Sir Keith Joseph. Although much derided by Labour and the Liberals at the time, the existence of a Cabinet minister with specific responsibility for Welsh matters undoubtedly fuelled demands for a further extension of separate governmental treatment, if not of devolution.

Yet, for all the prosperity of the time, the culture of Wales remained firmly dominated by Labour. In the general elections of 1955 and 1959, which saw the Conservatives increase their governmental majority substantially, Labour won twenty-seven Welsh seats each time. Furthermore, there were signs that Labour's long-held antagonism towards the separate political recognition of Wales, dating from the end of the First World War and the centralist ethic of Arthur Henderson and Sidney Webb at that time, was now changing. Although Labour had set its face against the so-called 'Parliament for Wales Campaign' in the early 1950s and had reprimanded MPs like Goronwy Roberts and S.O. Davies, the Merthyr Marxist, who endorsed it, it also recognized the need for government treating Wales less as a British region and more as a distinct nation. The unpopularity of Henry Brooke as minister for Welsh affairs in handling the controversy over the water resources of Tryweryn in Merioneth (A.4), when a beautiful north Wales valley was flooded to provide profitable supplies of water for the city of Liverpool, illustrated the dangers of London-based parties flouting local sentiment.

In 1959 Labour, much influenced by its then deputy leader James Griffiths, actually placed a secretary of state for Wales on its election manifesto for the first time (A.5). In the early 1960s,

A.3

A.4

A.5

this increased sensitivity for Welsh national needs, along with the growing unpopularity of the Macmillan (later Home) government, saw Labour's advance in Wales continue still further. In the general election of October 1964, when Labour narrowly returned to office under Harold Wilson, the party captured twenty-eight Welsh seats out of thirty-six, regaining Swansea West. In March 1966, Labour achieved the most triumphant success in its history in the principality, the zenith of its onward march. It captured thirty-two seats out of thirty-six, winning Cardiganshire from the Liberals (whose tally fell to just one), and Cardiff North, Conway and Monmouth from the Conservatives. The seal appeared to have been set on a Labour ascendancy, national and local, political and cultural, as rooted in Wales as had been the long years of Liberal ascendancy before 1914. The veteran James Griffiths became 'Charter Secretary of State'. From English incomers like James Callaghan and Michael Foot in south Wales to authentic Welsh-speaking figures like Cledwyn Hughes and Goronwy Roberts in the rural areas, afforced by Lady Megan Lloyd George who had transferred from a lifetime's family involvement with the Liberals, Labour's dominance appeared total and overwhelming. The pattern originally heralded in 1945 seemed fully confirmed.

In fact, Welsh politics were about to enter a quite different phase, one hard to detect prior to the early 1960s. This brought a new and passionate involvement with nationalism in all its forms. Until 1962, Welsh nationalism seemed to have made little enough headway. Plaid Cymru was a minor fringe movement politically, though influential in Welsh-language literary circles and within the University of Wales and the BBC. However, a new phase was heralded by a powerful broadcast, *Tynged yr Iaith* (The Fate of the Language) by the veteran, and highly controversial, nationalist littérateur, Saunders Lewis, on A.6   13 February 1962 (A.6). In this he called for militant methods to defend and preserve the Welsh language, a more significant cause than Welsh self-government itself, he claimed. 'Success is only possible through revolutionary methods,' Lewis declared.

This emotive appeal, coming at a time of protest and revolt amongst students and other young people in Europe and the United States, had a galvanizing effect. It led to a feeling that Labour hegemony in Wales, like the Liberal ascendancy in the past, was showing signs of becoming ingrown and sclerotic, and that perhaps the expectations aroused by the creation of the Welsh Office under James Griffiths (to be succeeded by Cledwyn Hughes in 1966 and then George Thomas in 1968) were not being fulfilled.

Quite unexpectedly, therefore, the politics of Wales were profoundly shaken by the upsurge of the previously minuscule Plaid Cymru. In July 1966 (following the death of Lady Megan Lloyd George), Gwynfor Evans, Plaid Cymru's president, captured Carmarthen from Labour, the first member of his party to be returned to Westminster. This had a dramatic impact on politics in the principality, especially among young people stirred by the excitements of the Welsh-language campaign. In response, the authorities, stubbornly insisting on the difficulty or impossibility of making government and legal business bilingual and of giving the Welsh language equal validity, seemed inert. With unemployment beginning to rise again in the later 1960s, Plaid Cymru naturally emerged as the obvious non-Tory alternative to entrenched Labour rule.

An election victory in Welsh-speaking, largely rural, Carmarthen was perhaps not so surprising. Much more remarkable were two further by-elections, in Rhondda West in March 1967 and in Caerphilly in July 1968. They were both rock-solid Labour strongholds where the party had maintained majorities of close to 20,000 and where Plaid had traditionally come nowhere. In Rhondda West, there was a 30 per cent swing to Plaid and Labour's majority fell from over 17,000 to 2,306. In Caerphilly, the swing to Plaid was nearly 40 per cent and Labour scraped home with a majority cut down to 1,874. Labour was deeply shaken by the collapse in its vote, organization and morale in traditional industrial strongholds. Richard Crossman's diary (A.7) records the shock of seeing Labour's empty committee room in Caerphilly just before the poll, manned only by the party's regional secretary, Emrys Jones. James Griffiths was told that 'you had better realize that all your

A.7

Gwynfor Evans arriving at Westminster following his victory in the Carmarthen by-election, 1966. (*Source: Plaid Cymru/National Library of Wales.*)

seats are marginal now', a somewhat exaggerated view but typical of the excitement produced by the nationalist upsurge in Wales, as also in Scotland in the later 1960s.

The political parties tried to respond in a variety of ways. One of the casualties was the Welsh Liberal Party, which had quite failed to find the capacity for renewal shown in England through the phenomenon of the suburban commuter, Orpington Man (and Woman). Its one MP now was Emlyn Hooson, member for Montgomeryshire, who was very active in promoting New Deal-type development programmes for the

A.8   regeneration of the rural economy of mid Wales (A.8). At the Welsh Office, Labour tried to provide new economic stimulus for Wales as a whole, notably through the White Paper *Wales,*

A.9   *the Way Ahead* (A.9), a classic restatement of the mixed-economy ethic of the 1960s, with extensive state intervention to provide for advance factories, trading estates and the public infrastructure.

A more emotive attempt to conciliate Welsh opinion came with the contrived investiture of Prince Charles as Prince of Wales at Caernarfon Castle on a sunny day in July 1969. This event, mercilessly satirized by the Welsh Language Society and by pop singers who sang derisively of 'Carlo', nevertheless had played a part in reinforcing unionist sentiment in Wales. Prince Charles himself had to undergo a crash course in Welsh during a summer term in Aberystwyth. At any rate, there were signs that nationalism might have passed its peak. In the June 1970 general election, Labour, although losing office, nevertheless maintained its dominant position in Wales with twenty-seven seats (and one Independent Labour) as against seven for the Conservatives and one Liberal. Gwynfor Evans was narrowly defeated in Carmarthen and the traditional pattern of Labour dominance appeared to be confirmed.

However, the nationalist upsurge, which had so widely permeated political culture in the 1960s, had left its mark. Indeed, there was one major potential time-bomb ticking for all the parties. This was the Crowther (later Kilbrandon) Royal Commission on the constitution, set up by Harold Wilson in 1968 as a counter to nationalist sentiment in Scotland and Wales. In October 1973 this commission duly reported. It produced a bewildering miscellany of reports and the impact on the public mind was confusing. However, what created the greatest impression was the fact that eleven of the thirteen members of the Kilbrandon Commission declared in favour of a Scottish legislative assembly, along with a more modest Welsh assembly with limited powers. Six of the eleven went further and called for a Welsh legislative assembly on the same basis as that for Scotland. Clearly, in view of the nation-wide pressure for a reassessment of the structure and government of the United Kingdom in response to Scottish and Welsh national demands, devolution was now centrally on the national agenda. For the first time since 1896, Welsh home rule in some form was a central priority.

The major parties responded somewhat hurriedly and half-heartedly. The Conservatives maintained a broadly unionist stance towards Wales: they had not greatly extended the authority of the Welsh Office during the years of the Heath government, 1970–4, while it was noted that its secretary of state for Wales, Peter Thomas, was actually member for Hendon South in suburban London. Labour regained office under Harold Wilson in March 1974, with such prominent Welsh representatives as James Callaghan and Michael Foot playing leading roles in the Cabinet, and other Welshmen such as Merlyn Rees, David Owen and Lord Elwyn-Jones, along with a 'Taffia' of junior ministers, active in the new administration. Labour and the unions stressed their commitment to traditional social and economic priorities: Labour had given broad support to the miners in the national coal strikes of February 1972 and February 1974, which played their part in undermining the Heath government. At the same time, devolution and nationalism would not go away. The new secretary of state for Wales, John Morris, was a committed devolutionist, assisted by such quasi-nationalist advisers as Gwilym Prys Davies. In the event, then, the 1970s, greatly affected by economic crisis, union troubles and industrial unrest, were also caught up with the long-running debate on Welsh devolution.

The government brought in a joint Devolution Bill for Wales

and Scotland in December 1976. Indeed, it was the prime minister, James Callaghan, who introduced it personally. The Welsh assembly would be a less powerful body than that in Scotland, with a block grant of £850 million for a new eighty-strong elected assembly, to be expended largely on social areas, but it was still a notable initiative. A derelict coal exchange in the Cardiff docks area was earmarked as the home for the putative new assembly. Plaid Cymru and some Labour and Liberal members felt committed to the new measure, sometimes passionately so. In Britain as a whole, however, there was a marked lack of enthusiasm, indeed a positive hostility from some English regions which felt that Wales and Scotland might well be unfairly favoured over themselves in regional aid programmes. The government's portmanteau devolution measure came to grief early in 1977, but a pact struck between the Labour government and the Liberals ensured that a minority administration would continue to plough on with the unrewarding task of pushing Welsh and Scottish devolution forward. Separate bills for Scotland and Wales were then introduced and, after immense difficulty, the Welsh devolution bill passed through all its stages in both houses and received the royal assent on 31 July 1978. Welsh self-government had never progressed so far before. But this was in many ways a deceptive landmark. The government had already had to concede referendums in both Scotland and Wales, while a Labour back-bencher's amendment laid down that 40 per cent of the electorate would have to vote 'yes' for the devolution measure to take effect, an almost impossible hurdle to surmount.

Labour exhibited divided counsels especially in industrialized, anglicized south Wales. Five rebel Labour MPs, headed by the youthful Neil Kinnock, member for Bedwellty, launched a campaign to have devolution rejected (A.10). Conversely, other Labour figures such as the secretary of state, John Morris, hailed devolution as a great step forward for local democracy and economic advance (A.11). But the referendum, held on St David's Day 1979, showed how unreal much of the euphoria surrounding devolution really was. The 'yes' campaign was largely a failure. Only 11.8 per cent (243,048) of the Welsh electorate voted for devolution, while 46.5 per cent (956,330)

A.10

A.11

voted against. Even in Welsh-speaking Gwynedd, which had elected Plaid Cymru MPs for Caernarfon and Merioneth in October 1974, there was an almost two-to-one vote against Welsh devolution. The entire affair set back the cause of nationalism for many years. It also played some part in undermining the beleaguered Labour government, already harassed by trade union militancy during the so-called 'winter of discontent' in 1978–9.

In the May 1979 general election, when James Callaghan's government was defeated, there was a 4.8 per cent swing to the Conservatives in Wales. Labour ended up with twenty-one seats, the Conservatives with eleven, Plaid Cymru with two and the Liberals with one (the speaker, George Thomas, was the other Welsh MP elected). Labour lost Brecon and Radnor and, more remarkably, Anglesey to the Conservatives. The Labour Party was manifestly collapsing in north and mid Wales, even in towns like Holyhead and Blaenau Ffestiniog. It looked and sounded like an elderly party, reminiscent of the corporate ethic of a previous era. Its local authorities were sometimes under fire for corrupt practices, effectively ventilated in such unofficial journals as *Rebecca*. Some prosecutions resulted in Swansea. Nicholas Edwards (Pembrokeshire), a Conservative of Anglican and business background, became the new secretary of state. An era in Welsh politics seemed to have come to its close.

From 1979 Welsh, as British, politics were dominated by the remarkable personality of Mrs Margaret Thatcher. It was a time of political polarization. Unemployment rose rapidly; coal-mines closed in swift succession until only one was left in south Wales by the end of 1993; monetarism and privatization were the dominant themes. At the same time, many responded to the ethic of enterprise and individual profit-making that Thatcherism embodied. Thus in 1983 the Conservatives made further progress in Wales, winning fourteen seats, their best result since 1895. Labour remained secure only in its industrial bastions, and its share of the vote fell to 37.5 per cent. If there was much deindustrialization, there was also inward investment in south Wales in the 1980s with new Japanese and other foreign firms

NATIONAL UNION OF MINEWORKERS (South Wales Area)

MacGregor's Democracy

NO-ONE ELECTED HIM. Appointed by Thatcher, he and his New York banking firm are being paid £3 million to destroy this country's energy industries.

Thatcher has already sold the British National Oil Corporation to MacGregor's friends in the City.

North Sea Gas is about to suffer the same fate. Power Station workers are being laid-off despite the fact that the Government has ordered the Electricity Board to import electricity from French nuclear stations via cross-channel cables.

Britain's coal is the next target. We have hundreds of years of reserves. Yet Thatcher would rather throw this country to the wolves who control the world energy markets.

In the next 12 months, she and MacGregor want to close 20 pits and shed 20,000 jobs. MacGregor told the NUM that over the next 3 years he wants to reduce the number of pits from 174 to 100 and the number of jobs from 180,000 to 100,000.

A further 160,000 jobs will disappear over the same period in industries supplying pits and carrying coal. This will hit engineering, rail and road transport, gas and electricity, not only in mining areas but throughout Britain.

These industries produce the wealth which pays for our public services. Without it, the health and education of our children and the welfare of our sick and aged will be placed in dire peril.

SAVE YOUR COMMUNITIES

SUPPORT THE MINERS

Leaflet published by the National Union of Mineworkers (South Wales Area) during the 1984–5 strike. (*Source: NUM South Wales Area.*)

providing economic stimulus in place of the declining staple industries of the past. Unemployment in Wales fell below the national average. The national miners' strike of 1984–5 was in some ways an embarrassment for the government's opponents. Miners' wives took an unprecedentedly prominent role (A.12). The miners in south Wales, although critical of Arthur Scargill and the NUM leadership's tactics, struggled and suffered together as they had done since the First World War. But it ended in a total defeat for the miners, and a political victory for the Thatcher government.

A.12

Meanwhile, the Welsh Office under Nicholas Edwards proved remarkably active and interventionist. One notable concession to local sentiment came in 1982 with the launch of a Welsh-language television channel, Sianel Pedwar Cymru (S4C), a cause for which the veteran Gwynfor Evans had threatened a hunger strike unto death, if necessary. Almost all aspects of social and economic life came under the control of the Welsh Office by the start of the 1990s, agriculture, health, housing, education, transport; its impact on all aspects of governance in the principality expanded considerably. A stimulus to the work of the office came with the advent of another Englishman, Peter Walker, as secretary of state for Wales. His 'Valleys Initiative' coincided with a surge of activity by the Welsh Development Agency in encouraging inward investment, notably from the Far East. The closeness of the 'M4 corridor' assisted south-east Wales. Later critics were to complain that the 'Valleys Initiative' was largely cosmetic and that the Welsh Development Agency's operations were marred by quasi-corrupt patronage and mismanagement. Wales remained a 'branch-factory economy' in most respects. Even so, under Peter Walker and his successor, David Hunt, the Welsh Office gave an impression of momentum and of interventionist government, somewhat at variance with the anti-statist philosophy of the Thatcher government itself (A.13).

A.13

It appeared for a time as if the Thatcher years would see Wales merge into a more generalized pattern of Conservative ascendancy. But in fact, however time-worn Labour might seem, however confined Plaid Cymru might be to the Welsh-speaking mountain fastnesses of the north and west, the decades-old tradition of radicalism retained its currency. Labour, now led by a Welshman, Neil Kinnock, emerged yet again as the natural voice of anti-Tory protest. It gained four seats from the Conservatives in the election of 1987, and in 1992 both Wales and Scotland showed a further swing away from the Conservative Party. In April 1992, under their new premier John Major, the Conservatives lost more ground in Wales. The results saw Labour winning twenty-seven of the seats with 49.5 per cent of the Welsh vote, as against six seats and 28.6 per cent for the Conservatives, four seats and 9 per cent of the vote for Plaid Cymru and just one for the Liberals, or Liberal Democrats as they were now known. The ephemeral 'Social Democrats' had vanished from the scene. Indeed, the 1992 election marked a further stage in the secular decline of the Welsh Liberals, since, with a mere 12.4 per cent of the Welsh vote, they polled less well in Wales than anywhere else in Britain. They reflected the politics of memory, rather than of hope. Labour, with gains in Cardiff Central, Pembrokeshire and Delyn in the north-east, kept the ascendancy they had maintained for seventy years.

The years since 1945 indicate a series of turning-points at which Welsh politics failed to turn. The apparently impregnable Labour ascendancy of the 1945–66 period, the nationalist upsurge in the late 1960s and early 1970s, the Thatcherite hegemony of the 1980s, all failed to last. The main distinctiveness of Welsh politics was expressed through the expansion of the Welsh Office and a variety of associated development and planning agencies. But these were, in a sense, made in Whitehall and imposed from outside. In the 1990s, the mass of unelected, largely unaccountable quangos, endorsed by a new right-wing secretary of state for Wales, John Redwood, sat curiously alongside the democratic radicalism of the Welsh political tradition. Authentic self-generating national pressure had not been politically effective. Against the success of cultural movements, such as the Welsh-schools movement and the language campaign, must be measured the general failure of political nationalism, evidenced spectacularly, perhaps cruelly, in the crushing defeat of Welsh devolution in 1979. In the early 1990s, Labour was again pledged to a Welsh elected assembly, but A.14   apart from specific groups of idealists and journalists (A.14), it was hard to see this cause attracting more enthusiasm than it had done previously throughout the twentieth century. Plaid Cymru had confirmed its presence along the western littoral from Anglesey to Cardiganshire, but its position in the industrial valleys and the populous south-east, never strong, had eroded markedly since the heady days of the late 1960s.

Welsh politics in the 1990s, as in Britain generally, displayed all the symptoms of a tradition in decay. The public mood was one of lethargy, perhaps of cynicism. Party membership was small and enthusiasm muted. Welsh politics did not appear to be throwing up figures of the stature of Bevan, James Griffiths or Cledwyn Hughes, let alone a Lloyd George, any more. Meanwhile, Welsh local government, the hub of politics since 1888, had, after twenty years of remodelling and the rate-capping of the Thatcher years, lost its impetus along with much of its power. Great local potentates like Llew Heycock of Port Talbot or Gwarnant Williams of Ceredigion need never have been. The Welsh had made their mark on modern Britain as a political nation no less than as a musical one — passionate, intense, articulate, creative. But in 1992, this seemed a world we had lost. Along with its coal-mines, chapels and choirs, the Welsh political culture, for the moment at least, seemed almost a part of archaeological 'heritage'. Like Big Pit at Blaenavon, it implied a nostalgic symbol of an immemorial, dying society. Only in 1995 did it seem that renewal might be at hand and a new era dawning.

Sources

A.1   The great day arrived. Before noon, we had one or two results coming in over the telephone and then throughout the afternoon we had the great bulk of reports available. My chart revealed that we were gaining seats in Wales and this gave me great delight and it would also give great pleasure to the many voluntary workers who had worked so hard in all parts of Wales during the campaign. As we entered the results on our chart we also kept in touch with our Head Office in London and they were able to give me, from time to time, a clear picture of what was happening throughout the country.

About mid-afternoon, when most of the results were known, I received a call from Mr Len Hill, our Election Agent for Mr George Dagger in the Abertillery constituency. I, of course, had already marked my chart with a sure win for this constituency because it was looked upon as a very safe Labour seat. However, over the telephone Len Hill started to apologise for being so late in giving the result and went on to explain that there had been a re-count. This shook me and I blurted out, 'What on earth went wrong in this safe seat for you to have a re-count?' Len replied 'Well, the Tory candidate just saved his deposit by a couple of hundred votes so we demanded a re-count to see if we could make him lose his deposit. That is why we are late, but we failed to make him lose his deposit.' I gave a sigh of relief but have on many occasions had a good laugh over that incident and indeed I could never understand why the Returning Officer granted a re-count. It also occurred to me that our people were not satisfied with inflicting a heavy defeat on the Tory candidate, they wanted to rub salt in the wound. The result of the poll in Abertillery was Mr George Dagger 28,615 and to the Tory candidate 4,422: it will be seen that the latter saved his deposit by less than two hundred votes. This is a very good story and perhaps it explains in some way the feelings at that time between supporters of the Labour Party and those of the Tory Party.

(Cliff Prothero, *Recount*, Ormskirk, Hesketh, 1982, pp.57–8.)

A.2   Administration of Wales and Monmouthshire: report by Herbert Morrison, 23 January 1946. CP(46) 21:

The proper remedy for Wales, as for Scotland, is to ensure that they both form part of a single economic plan for the whole country and are not thrown back on their own sectional resources.

Note by James Griffiths on the Area Board covering Wales under the Electricity Bill, 17 December 1946. CP(46) 462 :

The proposal to divide Wales in the Electricity Bill will be criticised both on grounds of National sentiment and on the grounds that they provide an arbitrary division of areas which, for other administrative purposes, are treated as a single unit.

Conclusions of Cabinet held on 15 October 1948:

(Herbert Morrison) The Welsh Regional Council of Labour, whose avowed aim was to obtain the appointment of a Minister for Welsh Affairs at some future date, had suggested that a Minister of Cabinet rank should preside over the Council, but the Committee were satisfied that this Ministerial Chairman would find himself in an embarrassing position and that the difficulties which would arise between him and other Ministers would strengthen the demand for a Secretary of State for Wales. It was accordingly proposed that individual Ministers of Cabinet rank should from time to time attend meetings of the Council, the choice of Minister depending on the main subject to be discussed.

(Cabinet Papers, Public Record Office.)

A.3   (Mr R.A. Butler)
There is only one other subject on which I wish to touch, and that is the very vexed question of how the administration of Wales is to be conducted. I will not disappoint the right hon. Gentleman by not mentioning the Secretary of State for Wales. It seems to me that a request for this comes partly from national pride, partly from a desire that Welsh needs shall not be overlooked, and partly from a feeling that Wales is being treated rather badly in comparison with Scotland. To dismiss this last comparison, it is obvious to everyone that the historical background and circumstances of Scotland and Wales are not identical; in fact, it would be very damaging to Wales to say it was identical with any other section of the world. Wales is something particular, and I believe some particular arrangement is necessary for Wales. What is wanted is not a muddling of the administration. I sympathise absolutely with what the present Chancellor said in the last Debate on the subject.

I agree absolutely with the Minister of Health that we do not want a Minister with over-riding powers. That, I believe, would lead to muddle. We do not want a messenger boy, to use one of the felicitous phrases of the Minister of Health. What we want is a watchdog, a Minister in the Government who can be, so to speak, an Ambassador for Wales who can, at the same time, watch and see that Wales is getting its fair share, and that the hon. Member for Abertillery supports his own government once in a while. That, at any rate, would be an achievement of any Minister who was interested. I suggest, not that we should have a Secretary of State in exactly the same way as we have a Secretary of State for Scotland.

. . . what I think absolutely necessary is a Minister who will watch the priorities and have some sort of vision in regard to Wales, whether by area, or as a whole, or North, or South, who will be forever present in the Cabinet as a watchdog for Wales, able to interest himself in the work of this committee of officials which has met in Cardiff and watch the co-ordination of the work done by the committee to which reference is made in the White Paper, and who has a special assignment to look after the case of Wales, and interest himself in it. I believe that that would be a most valuable addition to any Government. I do not absolutely insist that the person who holds it must be Welsh, but it would be a great advantage, whether he be Welsh or not, if he were full of that spirit which we always associate with that great country. I put forward that suggestion —

Mr S. O. Davies: Would the right hon. Gentleman's watchdog have anything other than a bark? . . .

Mr Butler: No, the hon. Member is putting his own construction on it. The dog I suggest would be complete in every respect. There will be other speakers on this side of the House, and I feel sure that they will develop further not only the point I have made, but also many other aspects of the life of rural Wales, to which I have referred.

I am convinced, after my close examination of this subject, that it is impossible to sunder the administration of Wales from that of England in major matters; secondly, that there is at present a great gap in policy as applied to Wales as a whole;

thirdly, that there is not a proper vision in the manner in which the benefits of policy are applied to the parts of Wales. The first step has been taken by this co-ordinating committee of officials. A further step ought now to be taken by someone of Ministerial status being put above that co-ordinating committee of officials. I believe that a scheme could be worked out which would be of great benefit to Wales and of advantage to both countries. I was reading the remarks of Mr Cowper Powys on Wales in *The Welsh Review*. He gives me great hope because he refers to Wales as 'the most conservative, the most introverted, the most mysterious nation that has ever existed on the earth . . .' It is because we are devoted to this nation and to her needs that I have taken up the time of the House this afternoon, and that right hon. and hon. Friends of mine wish also to take part and show their interest in this great subject .

(*Parliamentary Debates*, 5th series, 1946, Vol.446, cols.693–5.)

A.4   TRYWERYN

Liverpool Corporation's high-handedness on their plan for flooding Cwm Tryweryn has done more to arouse opposition in Wales than the plan itself. There is a feeling of anger which has nothing to do with nationalism. The main argument against the plan is simply that while Liverpool needs water for industrial purposes the city proposes to take it — and more besides, for re-sale, it is reported — from an area which has high hopes of attracting industries of its own in future.

If Merioneth water is piped away to Liverpool how can the local authority retain any of the bargaining power it will need to bring new industry into the county?

Liverpool Corporation is not the only local authority with a difficulty. Many Welsh county councils are faced with a far greater one, that of rural depopulation. The Tryweryn scheme, if carried out, will only aggravate this grave problem. This is a question not of nationalism but of pure common sense.

Plenty of water is left in Derwentwater, Grasmere, Windermere and other lakes in the region. Manchester gets its water from Haweswater in the Lake District.

A survey has deplored the loss of 8000 head of livestock, the partial afforestation of Tryweryn and the further squandering of precious farmland.

(*Western Mail*, leading article, 17 September 1956.)

A.5 In the years between 1945 and 1964, under successive governments, a number of steps were taken which, if not dramatic in their impact, yet led to a fuller consideration of, and increased opportunities to debate, Welsh affairs in Parliament . . .

Welcome as all these measures were, they did not satisfy the desire for fuller recognition of our nationhood nor the demand for devolution of administration. While I had opposed the proposal for a Parliament for Wales, I was convinced that both on grounds of national sentiment and the necessity for further devolution of administration, the appointment of a Secretary of State and the creation of a Welsh Office were desirable. The majority of the Welsh local authorities and the Welsh Council of Labour had declared their support for this proposal.

Hitherto the majority of my colleagues in the Labour Party had been opposed. However, a fresh opportunity came to give further consideration to the question when in readiness for the 1959 election the National Executive of the party set up a special committee, under my chairmanship, to prepare a Labour programme for Wales. I was, at the time, the deputy leader of the party and I had discussions with Hugh Gaitskell and my Welsh colleagues and urged them to agree to include it in the programme.

To my intense satisfaction they unanimously agreed and for the first time the Labour Party pledged itself to include a Secretary of State for Wales in the next Labour Government. When Hugh Gaitskell came to our Welsh Labour conference and added his pledge as leader of the party it was received with enthusiasm. The pledge was reaffirmed in the 1964 manifesto and by Harold Wilson at Cardiff in his first speech as leader.

(James Griffiths, *Pages from Memory*, London, Dent, 1969, pp.164–5.)

A.6 A ydy'r sefyllfa'n anobeithiol? Ydy', wrth gwrs, os bodlonwn ni i anobeithio. 'Does dim yn y byd yn fwy cysurus nag an-obeithio. Wedyn gall dyn fynd ymlaen i fwynhau byw.

Y mae traddodiad politicaidd y canrifoedd, y mae holl dueddiadau economaidd y dwthwn hwn, yn erbyn parhad y Gymraeg. Ni all dim newid hynny ond penderfyniad, ewyllys, brwydro, aberth, ymdrech. A gaf i alw eich sylw chi at hanes Mr. a Mrs. Trefor Beasley. Glowr yw Mr. Beasley. Yn Ebrill 1952 prynodd ef a'i wraig fwthyn yn Llangennech gerllaw Llanelli, mewn ardal y mae naw o bob deg o'i phoblogaeth yn Gymry Cymraeg. Yn y cyngor gwledig y perthyn Llangennech iddo y mae'r cynghor-wyr i gyd yn Gymry Cymraeg: felly hefyd swyddogion y cyngor. Gan hynny, pan ddaeth papur hawlio'r dreth leol atynt oddi wrth *The Rural District Council of Llanelly*, anfonodd Mrs. Beasley i ofyn am ei gael yn Gymraeg. Gwrthodwyd. Gwrthododd hithau dalu'r dreth nes ei gael. Gwysiwyd hi a Mr. Beasley dros ddwsin o weithiau gerbron llys yr ustusiaid. Mynnodd Mr. a Mrs. Beasley fod dwyn y llys ymlaen yn Gymraeg. Tair gwaith bu'r beilïod yn cludo dodrefn o'u tŷ nhw, a'r dodrefn yn werth llawer mwy na'r dreth a hawlid. Aeth hyn ymlaen am wyth mlynedd. Yn 1960 cafodd Mr. a Mrs. Beasley bapur dwy-ieithog yn hawlio'r dreth leol oddi wrth Gyngor Dosbarth Gwledig Llanelli, a Chymraeg y bil lawn cystal â'i Saesneg. Nid oes gennyf i hawl i ddweud beth a gostiodd hyn oll yn ariannol i Mr. a Mrs. Beasley. Bu cyfeillion yn lew iawn, gan gynnwys cyfreith-wyr a bargyfreithwyr. Aeth eu helynt yn destun sylw gwlad, a'r papurau newydd a'r radio a'r teledu yn boen beunyddiol iddynt. Yr oedd yr achosion yn y llys yn ddiddorol a phwysig. Er enghraifft, ateb swyddog y dreth i Mr. Wynne Samuel: 'Nid oes unrhyw rwymedigaeth ar y Cyngor i argraffu'r papurau sy'n hawlio'r dreth mewn unrhyw iaith ond Saesneg.'

Yng nghanol y rhyfel diwethaf, yn Hydref 1941, trwy ymdrech bwysicaf Undeb Cymru Fydd, cyflwynwyd deiseb i'r Senedd, deiseb y torrodd tua phedwar can mil o Gymry eu henwau wrthi, yn erfyn am ddeddf 'A wna'r Iaith Gymraeg yn unfraint â'r Iaith Saesneg ym mhob agwedd ar Weinyddiad y Gyfraith a'r Gwasanaethau Cyhoeddus yng Nghymru'. Ond wedi'r llafur mawr a'r hel enwau a chynadleddau aeth yr aelodau seneddol Cymreig i gyfrinachu â Mr. Herbert Morrison, yr Ysgrifennydd Cartref ar y pryd. Y canlyniad fu'r *Welsh Courts*

Act, 1942, deddf seneddol a ddiystyrodd holl fwriad y ddeiseb ac a adawodd y Saesneg o hyd yn unig iaith swyddogol y llysoedd cyfraith a'r gwasanaethau cyhoeddus oll. At hynny y cyfeiriodd swyddog y dreth yn Llanelli.

Fe ellir achub y Gymraeg. Y mae Cymru Gymraeg eto'n rhan go helaeth o ddaear Cymru ac nid yw'r lleiafrif eto'n gwbl ddibwys. Dengys esiampl Mr. a Mrs. Beasley sut y dylid mynd ati. Trwy wyth mlynedd ymdrech Mrs. Beasley, un Cymro arall yn y dosbarth gwledig a ofynnodd am bapur y dreth yn Gymraeg. Peth na ellir ei wneud yn rhesymol ond yn unig yn y rhannau hynny y mae'r Cymry Cymraeg yn nifer sylweddol o'r boblogaeth yw hyn. Eler ati o ddifri a heb anwadalu i'w gwneud hi'n amhosibl dwyn ymlaen fusnes llywodraeth leol na busnes llywodraeth ganol heb y Gymraeg. Hawlier fod papur y dreth yn Gymraeg neu yn Gymraeg a Saesneg. Rhoi rhybudd i'r Postfeistr Cyffredinol na thelir trwyddedau blynyddol oddieithr eu cael yn Gymraeg. Mynnu fod pob gŵys i lys yn Gymraeg. Nid polisi i unigolion, un yma, un acw ar siawns mo hyn. Byddai gofyn ei drefnu a symud o gam i gam gan roi rhybudd a rhoi amser i gyfnewidiadau. Polisi i fudiad yw ef a'r mudiad hwnnw yn yr ardaloedd y mae'r Gymraeg yn iaith lafar feunyddiol ynddynt. Hawlio fod pob papur etholiad a phob ffurflen swyddogol yn ymwneud ag etholiadau lleol neu seneddol yn Gymraeg. Codi'r Gymraeg yn brif fater gweinyddol y dosbarth a'r sir.

Efallai y dywedwch chi na ellid hynny fyth, na cheid fyth ddigon o Gymry i gytuno ac i drefnu'r peth yn ymgyrch o bwys a grym. 'Hwyrach eich bod yn iawn. Y cwbl a ddaliaf i yw mai dyna'r unig fater politicaidd y mae'n werth i Gymro ymboeni ag ef heddiw. Mi wn yr anawsterau. Byddai'n stormydd o bob cyfeiriad. Fe daerid fod y cyfryw ymgyrch yn lladd ein siawns i ddenu ffatrïoedd Seisnig i'r ardaloedd gwledig Cymraeg; a diau mai felly y byddai. Hawdd addo y byddai gwawd a dirmyg y sothach newyddiadurwyr Saesneg yn llaes feunyddiol. Byddai dig swyddogion yr awdurdodau lleol a llawer cyngor sir yn ail i'r bytheirio a fu yn Nosbarth Gwledig Llanelli. Byddai'r dirwyon yn y llysoedd yn drwm, ac o wrthod eu talu byddai'r canlyniadau'n gostus, er nad yn fwy costus nag ymladd etholiadau seneddol diamcan. Nid wyf yn gwadu na byddai cyfnod o gas ac erlid a chynnen yn hytrach na'r cariad heddychol sydd mor amlwg ym mywyd politicaidd Cymru heddiw. Nid dim llai na chwyldroad yw adfer yr iaith Gymraeg yng Nghymru. Trwy ddulliau chwyldro yn unig y mae llwyddo. Efallai y dygai'r iaith hunan-lywodraeth yn ei sgil; 'wn i ddim. Mae'r iaith yn bwysicach na hunan-lywodraeth. Yn fy marn i, pe ceid unrhyw fath o hunan-lywodraeth i Gymru cyn arddel ac arfer yr iaith Gymraeg yn iaith swyddogol yn holl weinyddiad yr awdurdodau lleol a gwladol yn y rhanbarthau Cymraeg o'n gwlad, ni cheid mohoni'n iaith swyddogol o gwbl, a byddai tranc yr iaith yn gynt nag y bydd ei thranc hi dan Lywodraeth Loegr.

(Saunders Lewis, *Tynged yr Iaith*, London, BBC, 1962, pp.26–30)

(Is the position hopeless? It is, of course, if we are content to give up hope. For then one can go on to enjoy life.

The political tradition of the centuries and all present-day economic tendencies militate against the continued existence of Welsh. Nothing can change that except determination, will-power, struggle, sacrifice and endeavour. May I call your attention to the story of Mr. and Mrs. Trefor Beasley? Mr. Beasley is a coal-miner. In April 1952 he and his wife bought a cottage in Llangennech near Llanelli, a district where nine out of every ten of the population are Welsh-speaking. All the councillors on the rural council which controls Llangennech are Welsh-speaking: so too are the council officials. Therefore when a note demanding the local rates arrived from 'The Rural District Council of Llanelly' Mrs. Beasley wrote to ask for it in Welsh. It was refused. She refused to pay the rates until she got it. She and Mr. Beasley were summoned more than a dozen times to appear before the magistrates' court. Mr. and Mrs. Beasley insisted that the court proceedings should be in Welsh. Three times did the bailiffs carry off furniture from their home, the furniture being worth much more than the rates which were demanded. This went on for eight years. In 1960 Mr. and Mrs. Beasley received a bilingual note demanding the local rates from 'Cyngor Dosbarth Gwledig Llanelli', the Welsh on the bill being just as good as its English. It is not my right to say what was the financial cost of all this to Mr. and Mrs. Beasley.

Friends, including solicitors and barristers, were very loyal. Their trouble became the subject of the country's attention, and the newspapers and radio and television plagued them continually. The court cases were interesting and important. For example, the rating officer's reply to Mr. Wynne Samuel: 'The Council is not under any obligation to print rate-demand notes in any language except English.'

In the middle of the last war, in October 1941 — as a result of Undeb Cymru Fydd's (Union of the Wales to Be) most important campaign — a petition was presented to Parliament, a petition signed by approximately four hundred thousand Welshmen, appealing for a law placing the Welsh language on a footing of equality with the English language in all proceedings connected with the Administration of Justice and Public Services in Wales.

But after the great labour, the collection of signatures, and the conferences, the Welsh members of Parliament went into conclave with Mr. Herbert Morrison, the Home Secretary at the time. The result was the Welsh Courts Act of 1942, a parliamentary Act which disregarded the whole purpose of the petition and which still left English as the only official language of the courts and all the public services. That was what the Llanelli rating officer was referring to.

The Welsh language can be saved. Welsh-speaking Wales is still quite an extensive part of Wales territorially, and the minority is not yet wholly unimportant. The example of Mr. and Mrs. Beasley shows how we should set about it. During Mrs. Beasley's eight years of endeavour only one other Welshman in the rural district asked for a rate demand in Welsh. This cannot be done reasonably except in those districts where Welsh speakers are a substantial proportion of the population. Let us set about it in seriousness and without hesitation to make it impossible for the business of local and central government to continue without using Welsh. Let it be insisted upon that the rate demand should be in Welsh or in Welsh and English. Let the Postmaster-General be warned that annual licences will not be paid unless they are obtainable in Welsh. Let it be insisted upon that every summons to a court should be in Welsh. This is not a chance policy for individuals here and there. It would demand organizing and moving step by step, giving due warn-

ing and allowing time for changes. It is a policy for a movement, and that a movement in the areas where Welsh is the
spoken language in daily use. Let it be demanded that every
election communication and every official form relating to local
or parliamentary elections should be in Welsh. Let Welsh be
raised as the chief administrative issue in district and county.

Perhaps you will say that this could never be done, that not
enough Welshmen could be found to agree and to organize it as
a campaign of importance and strength. Perhaps you are right.
All I maintain is that this is the only political matter which it is
worth a Welshman's while to trouble himself about today. I
know the difficulties. There would be storms from every direction. It would be argued that such a campaign was killing our
chances of attracting English factories to the Welsh-speaking
rural areas, and that would doubtless be the case. It is easy to
predict that the scorn and sneers of the English gutter journalist
would be a daily burden. The anger of local authority officials
and those of many county councils would be like the blustering
of those in the Llanelli Rural District. Fines in courts would be
heavy, and a refusal to pay them would bring expensive consequences, though no more expensive than fighting
purposeless parliamentary elections. I do not deny that there
would be a period of hatred, persecution and controversy in
place of the brotherly love which is so manifest in Welsh political life today. It will be nothing less than a revolution to restore
the Welsh language in Wales. Success is only possible through
revolutionary methods. Perhaps the language would bring self-
government in its wake — I don't know. In my opinion, if any
kind of self-government for Wales were obtained before the
Welsh language was acknowledged and used as an official
language in local authority and state administration in the
Welsh-speaking parts of our country, then the language would
never achieve official status at all, and its demise would be
quicker than it will be under English rule.)

(Translated by G. Aled Williams, BBC Publications, February
1962.)

George Thomas, Labour candidate for Cardiff West, talking to voters outside the Grand Avenue Polling Station in Ely during the 1964 General Election campaign. (*Source: Western Mail & Echo Ltd.*)

A.7   Thursday, 18 July 1968

Although Harold was complimentary enough I knew that the whole of my paper was completely useless, two years too late. Ironically, today was the day of the Caerphilly by-election. As I was chatting to George Thomas before this meeting, he told me that he'd just come back from there. Last night, he said, he had gone into the Central Committee Rooms after his eve-of-poll meeting and found there Emrys Jones, the Regional Organizer, sitting alone. That's an eye-opener. When one thinks of the bustle, the cups of tea and everybody saying, 'My God, this is a marvellous campaign' and the people pouring in and out of the room which is normal in any well-organized by-election and then thinks of this one person sitting alone it's terrifying. Certainly George Thomas was terrified and he told me that we weren't going to win. Three times this evening when we were talking about devolution the P.M. turned to me and said, 'We'd better write off Caerphilly. I'm afraid we've lost it.' I knew he was arranging some psychological insurance against defeat, acclimatizing himself to the disaster before it hit him. My mind was on devolution and the more I thought about the major onslaught which is going to overwhelm us the less adequate my proposals seemed to be.

(Richard Crossman, *The Diaries of a Cabinet Minister, Vol.3, Secretary of State for Social Services, 1968–70*, London, Hamilton Cape, 1977, p.145.)

A.8   The over-all picture of Mid-Wales in 1965 therefore is not a happy one and, while it is an area of great natural beauty, it is occupied by a declining and increasingly elderly population. The proportion of people employed is well below average; the employment in agriculture is declining and only a very limited number can find work in forestry and in the too few light industries remaining in the region. In the country, as in the towns, remunerative work is the foundation upon which the rest of life is built. Without work there can be no facilities for civilised living, neither can there be an expression of culture. In the landscape of Mid-Wales today, evidence of depopulation is everywhere apparent, and reminders of more prosperous days may be seen in every county. In the hills may be found the ruined remains of countless farmhouses and cottages; there are completely deserted villages of once dynamic and live communities; even in the towns one may still stumble across the remains of tanneries or textile factories. Those people that remain in Mid-Wales populate an area where public services, communications and amenities generally fall well below the standards that they are entitled to expect in the middle of the 20th century.

Those who care for the future of Wales, or indeed for the future of the rural areas of Britain as a whole, must face these problems. Conditions in Mid-Wales must be so changed that there is no need for the majority of young people to drift across Offa's Dyke in search of work. The drift from the land must be arrested; the population must be increased and a livelihood provided for young people so that they each take their rightful place in the community.

The Plan

Phase I

In essence the main aims during the first phase are as follows:

(a) Developing the basic industry of agriculture.

(b) Developing the existing towns of Mid-Wales and establishing village clusters around market towns.

(c) Laying down a modern system of roads and preserving essential rail communications.

1. The Group is already working on a full-scale study of the future of Welsh agriculture, and it is recognised that ultimately the strength of the agricultural industry depends upon national policy. Agriculture is the basic industry of Mid-Wales and it is essential to take urgent steps to strengthen its foundations. We believe that it is in the national interest that as much food as possible should be produced at home; and there is considerable

scope for further increasing the agricultural production and improving agricultural methods both in husbandry and marketing . . .

2. In this first phase of planning, a certain amount of industry must be introduced into Mid-Wales towns. The development may be envisaged as follows:

The Government should immediately bring in a small amendment to the Local Employment Act 1960, as amended in 1963. This amendment should be framed so as to enable some areas of depopulation to be scheduled as development districts. Once that is done then the whole of Mid-Wales should be so scheduled . . .

A Rural Development Corporation would be set up and would act as the agent of the Board of Trade and of the Welsh Office. Its first task would be to mobilise leadership and to co-ordinate development with a view to rehabilitating the whole of Mid-Wales.

(Emlyn Hooson and Geraint Jenkins, *The Heartland: A Plan for Mid-Wales*, New Directions, London, 1965, pp.8–11.)

A.9   PART FIVE — APPRAISAL

395.   An essential first step in planning for the development of Wales is to examine all the main fields of economic and social activity and the different areas of the Principality, in order to establish the nature of the problems that have to be solved. The purpose of the White Paper is to do this, and against that background, to review the Government's present policies for Wales.

The Employment Problem

396.   The foremost problem is how to make fuller use of the human resources that are available. During the past decade, the overall demand for male labour has been static and less than the supply. Despite the substantial progress which has been

made in the diversification of the economy, the Principality is
still very much dependent upon the traditional industries of
coal mining and steel; and, although employment opportunities
in new manufacturing industry and in service industries have
rapidly increased, those for males have not quite offset the
reduction in opportunities in these two traditional industries, in
agriculture and in slate quarrying. Consequently there is relatively high unemployment and a loss of younger people by
migration. Too many of the self-employed men have low
incomes. The number of women in employment has been
increasing rapidly, but the proportion is still low as compared
with other parts of Great Britain. It is this inadequate number
of employment opportunities which accounts for the comparat-
ively low level of per capita income and the relatively high
dependence of the Welsh economy on assistance from the
Exchequer and on the import of capital (Chapter I and
Paragraphs 78–91).

397.   Any calculation of the scale of the need for additional
jobs is bound to be imprecise, based as it must be on factors
which cannot be accurately measured and on assumptions
which future events may falsify. In paragraphs 93 to 100 there is
a calculation, made in March 1967, of the amount of labour
likely to be effectively available for employment in 1971,
compared with the estimated opportunities for employment
in that year. It was made, on the best information available, in
order to provide an indication of the order of magnitude of the
employment problem in the Principality, and thus give a
basis for policy. This calculation suggested, on the basis of policies as they existed in March 1967, the prospects then in sight,
and the assumptions made, that the supply of and demand for
female labour might be in balance in 1971 at a higher level than
at present; but that there might be an excess of something of
the order of 15,000 males effectively available for employment
over the employment opportunities for them. This estimate
allowed for the decline in employment in some industries and
the growth expected in others, for the expected natural increase
in population, and for an increase in the numbers in schools
and colleges. It assumed no net migration, with a declining

loss of younger people and an increasing immigration of older ones.

398.   Since this calculation was made in March 1967, the Government have already taken a number of decisions which should serve to improve the position as it was then forecast. The most important of these decisions was that to introduce a Regional Employment Premium for manufacturing industry in Development Areas, and the legislative provision necessary for its introduction has been included in the Finance Bill. The scheme will continue for at least seven years. It should provide material encouragement to industrial expansion in Development Areas, including Wales, and should have a substantial effect in increasing employment opportunities there. The adoption of this scheme will be followed by a study which will cover the problems of districts adjacent to Development Areas in which the rate of economic growth may give cause for concern. Further decisions taken since March 1967 are referred to below. They include a decision, taken partly in pursuance of a policy of seeking to steer major new development to those parts of the Wales Development Area which are within commuting distance of localities where the largest unemployment difficulties are likely to exist, to appoint consultants to advise on urban growth in the Llantrisant area and its neighbourhood. They also include decisions to establish the Royal Mint at Llantrisant and the Ministry of Transport motor vehicle licensing and goods vehicles test booking establishments at Swansea; and to construct additional advance factories (Paragraphs 171 to 177).

The Areas of Wales

408.   The economic problems of Wales vary greatly in their nature and intensity as between the different parts of Wales, and the policies of the Government for the deployment of the resources available in the most advantageous manner to meet those problems can most easily be summarised on a geographical basis.

South-East Wales

409.   Cardiff, Newport and the part of Monmouthshire
outside the valleys form an area which already possesses a
substantial and diversified industrial base, and has great poten-
tialities for further rapid economic growth. It was excluded
from the Wales Development Area created in 1966, because the
natural exploitation of its own geographical strength should
ensure its yet greater prosperity (Paragraph 157).

410.   The policies of the Government for this area are
mainly directed at improving communications, ports and other
services; at building up offices and similar establishments
including those dispersed from congested areas; and at ensuring that new development is carefully sited and that outworn
urban areas are redeveloped on attractive lines. The Severn
Bridge, the Ross Spur M50 Motorway and the road of near-
motorway standard under construction to link this with
Newport; the prospective completion of the M5 Motorway
between Bristol and the Midlands and of the M4 Motorway
between Newport and London; fast passenger rail services with
London and the introduction of liner trains, should make the
whole area even more attractive than at present to new manufacturing industry. New Government offices, some on a
substantial scale, are being established in Cardiff and Newport.
The development of parts of Cardiff in the light of the
Buchanan studies should increase further the attractions of the
capital city. The greater part of Monmouthshire will form part
of the area to be covered by a feasibility study of the growth
potential of the whole of the Severnside area which has been
set on foot (Paragraphs 343 and 345).

North-East Wales

411.   This area also possesses a sound existing industrial
base, notably in its steel, textile, chemical and aircraft plants;
and it offers advantages for further industrial development
because of its proximity to the Midlands and Merseyside.
Except for Wrexham and its vicinity, which has been affected

by colliery closures, it was excluded from the Wales Development Area in 1966. The main need is for an improvement of communications and services, careful planning control of new development, the improvement by clearance of derelict land and the development of some of the outworn urban areas and town centres. A proposal for a barrage across the Dee estuary which would connect the area by road with Merseyside is under examination and a first stage feasibility study report has already been prepared and is under review by the Government (Paragraphs 349–356).

The Mining Valleys and West South Wales

412.   In terms of numbers the inadequacy of employment opportunities is likely to be greatest in the mining valleys and the Swansea area. Where suitable sites attractive to industry are available, the Government will encourage the establishment of further new industries in the valleys themselves, and have already constructed there a number of advance factories at the expense of the Government as an attraction to tenants. But the shortage of sites and the locational shortcomings of the valleys gravely limit what can be done in this way. Reliance must, therefore, be largely placed on establishing new opportunities for employment within reasonable daily travelling distance. This will enable the existing investment in the valleys in houses, schools and other services to continue to be put to use (Paragraphs 335–341).

413.   The Government have under consideration a proposal for a major new urban development in an area already attractive to industry close to the mouths of the Rhondda and Taff valleys. An industrial estate is being set up at Llantrisant and it is at Llantrisant that the Royal Mint is to be established. A new urban focus in that area could house a fair part of the future increase of population in South Wales. It would provide employment opportunities for persons living in the neighbouring valleys, reduce the pressure to develop on the periphery of Cardiff and on the coast, and encourage those who wish to leave the valleys not to leave Wales. As an immediate first step,

the Government are appointing consultants to advise on the desirable future scale, timing, layout, cost and organisation of urban growth in the Llantrisant area and its neighbourhood (Paragraph 342). Relevant in this connection will be the timing and phasing of a new road through Mid-Glamorgan which will be needed from the present end of the M4 Motorway at Newport to the Bridgend area, and which would also provide an outer by-pass to Cardiff (Paragraphs 50(e) and 346).

414.   The Government are similarly encouraging the creation of new employment in the Swansea–Llanelli area, which will be made more attractive to industrialists by the road improvements already programmed. As part of the policy of dispersing offices, a Land Registry will be established at Swansea. An important decision is that of the Ministry of Transport to set up there the new national motor vehicle licensing office, computer centre, and goods vehicle test booking office for all Great Britain (Paragraphs 344, 169 and 176).

415.   Both in the mining valleys and in the Swansea area, vigorous action is in hand to rehabilitate derelict land and improve the environment. The Government attach importance to early action to clear the derelict area at Landore in the lower Swansea valley (Paragraphs 271–276).

Rural Wales

416.   Particular encouragement is given through the price support system to the production of meat, and this is of special value to Welsh farmers who obtain two-thirds of their receipts from livestock products. Under the Agriculture Act 1967, financial assistance will be given for desirable amalgamation of farms, which will reduce the number of uneconomic smallholdings, and other assistance of special value to Welsh farmers raising livestock on hill land. A Rural Development Board will be set up under the Act in Mid-Wales to co-ordinate the development of agriculture and forestry. Encouragement will also be given to the fishing industry and to forestry (Paragraphs 105–125).

417. Tourism in Wales has great potential for further growth, and this is most encouraging for the economy of the rural areas and coastal towns of Wales. The Government have increased their financial contribution to the Wales Tourist Board, through the British Travel Association. It is important that the local authorities and the Welsh tourist interests should also increase their support for the Board and provide improved facilities for tourists. Careful planning control will be needed to ensure that the amenities which attract tourists are not affected by ill-designed or ill-sited development. New access routes across the Severn Bridge, and possibly later on across the Dee estuary, may present problems and opportunities different in scale from anything so far experienced and a strategy must be worked out to meet them (Paragraphs 139–146).

418. A main spur to the economy of the rural areas must, however, be new small scale manufacturing industry in suitable places, and the incentives available under the Industrial Development Act 1966 and the Regional Employment Premium will help to attract it. A Mid-Wales Development Corporation is being set up under the New Towns Act with, as its immediate task, doubling the size of Newtown. Studies are also being made of the possibility of expanding Rhayader and some other towns to provide focal points for economic and social development (Paragraphs 365–370).

Coastal Towns

419. The coastal towns will benefit from the development of tourism and in particular from the improvements planned to the roads which serve them. They are attracting some new manufacturing enterprises, and in West Wales the rapidly growing oil refining industry and the associated production of petro-chemicals are taking advantage of the deep water facilities for large tankers at Milford Haven.

(*Wales: The Way Ahead*, HMSO, Cmd. 3334, July 1967, pp.122ff.)

A.10   M.P.s give 10 reasons for voting No

ANTI-DEVOLUTION GROUP SAY ASSEMBLY POSES GREAT
THREATS

By David G. Rosser, Political Editor

Wales can afford neither the risks nor the costs involved in
having its own elected Assembly, the six anti-devolution Welsh
Labour M.P.s said yesterday.

The Government's proposals posed great economic and
social threats and gambles for the people of Wales and, if implemented, would also threaten the unity of Wales, the United
Kingdom and the Labour movement, they said in London.

The six made it clear they intended to fight a tough campaign
against both the all-party Wales for the Assembly Campaign
and the Labour/Welsh TUC pro-Assembly group, but will be
independent of the umbrella No to the Assembly Campaign.

They are Mr. Leo Abse (Pontypool), Mr. Ifor Davies (Gower),
Mr. Fred Evans (Caerphilly), Mr. Ioan Evans (Aberdare), Mr.
Donald Anderson (Swansea East), and Mr. Neil Kinnock
(Bedwellty). Wales's 16 other Labour M.P.s back the Assembly.

In a formidable 10-point document entitled Facts to Beat the
Fantasies, the six say they are anxious to correct what they call
the false claims of the Vote Yes campaigners.

Compiled as a joint effort by the M.P.s it will be sent to
county conveners and stewards throughout Wales and will be
available, but not directly on offer, to the umbrella No to the
Assembly Campaign. The M.P.s insist this is their own and
separate effort to put across the disadvantages to Wales of an
Assembly.

It states: 'After the most thorough examination of the
proposals over the past three-and-a-half years and taking into
account the realities of modern economics and modern politics
we believe these proposals, if put into effect, would impose
costs the people of Wales cannot afford to pay, risks they
cannot afford to take, conflict with the rest of Britain and
disharmony within Wales which they do not want.'

A new level of government would not serve either their

Front page of the *South Wales Echo*, 2 March 1979. (*Source: Western Mail & Echo Ltd.*)

democratic needs, their community purposes or their pockets, purses or pension books.

But the M.P.s' most emphatic concern is that Wales would not survive as a community or as a culture if it further crippled itself with the unwanted and unnecessary burdens of expense and disunity that would result from the Assembly.

Denouncing the 'Yes-men' as the guessmen whose claims had not and could not be substantiated, the document poses the nub of the issue as, 'Will the Assembly bring advantage or disadvantage to the ordinary people of Wales?'

(*Western Mail*, 7 February 1979.)

A.11   Assembly will provide jobs boost, claims manifesto

By John Osmond, Welsh Affairs Correspondent

At Shotton last night, the Secretary of State for Wales, Mr. John Morris, said the No campaigners had inflated the costs of setting up the Assembly. 'The cost of a halfpenny per person per week to get better decisions and more participation by people from all over Wales is well worth it,' he said.

Mr. Morris said the powers of local government would not be affected by the Assembly. 'There is no reduction in the financial resources of local government,' he said.

He added that at present there was great dissatisfaction because the needs of particular areas in Wales were lost in the rate support grant calculations for England and Wales together. 'With direct negotiations, and a smaller number of institutions, direct effect would be given to local needs like unemployment or sparse population,' he said.

Mechanism

By improving and making more acceptable decisions made in Wales, the Assembly would strengthen and not fracture the unity of the United Kingdom, said Mr. Morris.

Mr. Morris said there was no basis in the No campaigners' claim that Wales might lose more than £1,000m. a year as a result of the Assembly. Although the mechanism for deciding public expenditure would change, Wales's share would continue to be based on need.

Mr. Morris said the No campaigners had simply not provided any evidence for their claim that the Assembly would risk central Government financial assistance to Wales.

He said the Assembly proposals were not a sellout to nationalism. 'Anyone who has participated in the Labour movement in Wales, both in our conferences and the Wales TUC, will know the present proposals have been under discussion since 1966,' he added.

(*Western Mail*, 8 February 1979)

A.12 Beneath the smooth, united surface of the Maerdy strikers, there are many tensions between wife and husband caused by partners stretching against the limits of 'acceptable behaviour'. Around Christmas time, according to one woman:

'The men became concerned that the women were taking a more stringent role in the striking . . . the women were reaching the ordinary man and woman in the street more than the men with their speaking about the day-to-day things of the strike. The men were a bit worried that we weren't going to be the same. Now things are on a more even keel. They can see we're not going to run off and split the families and demand equal rights for women.'

Women in Maerdy will say that they have sorted out the domestic duties with their husbands but really things are not so simple. There are rows about who's going out and who's going to babysit, who's going off on a speaking engagement and for how long. Women say that since the beginning of the dispute they share the cooking and cleaning but I have never seen a man do either in Maerdy. The burden is still on the woman to plan and organise the home although it is possible that men are taking on more than before.

It seems from talking to men that most of them draw a sharp line between the strike-based activity of the women, which they think of as good and useful, and other kinds of female militancy which they see as bad and unnatural. The point at which the women's group begins to affect the running of the house is the point at which many become frightened of 'the fems' and spend a lot of time talking about them. It almost goes without saying that it is an eye opener for them to meet, often, middle-class feminists with radically different lifestyles from their own.

Maerdy miners who were billeted with one woman in Oxford would come home at weekends with tales that she would 'rather build a wall in the garden than wash a cup'. The Oxford woman's argument was that she had spent enough years of her life serving men and that, when guests appear, she doesn't mind looking after the women but the men can pour their own tea. The miners claim to be deeply offended. It breaks every rule of Welsh hospitality they say, and the whole thing has turned into a usually jokey battle between the two sides with the miners trying to wind her up by singing songs like: 'Get into that kitchen and rattle those pots and pans . . .'

(Barbara Bloomfield, 'Women's Support Group at Maerdy', in Raphael Samuel, Barbara Bloomfield and Guy Boanas (eds.), *The Enemy Within: Pit Villages and the Miners' Strike of 1984–5*, London, Routledge and Kegan Paul, 1986, pp.161ff.)

A.13   Quite separate was the Valleys Initiative. I said we were going to have to clean up the valleys and adopt a range of measures. To announce them individually was silly. What we should do was to look at what we could and needed to do over the next three years, putting all the plans together in one document, so that people could see what was going to happen and when. Derelict land clearance, road building, new schools, new hospitals were to be listed. I pulled together the details of what each section of the department thought it could do and wrote the document myself.

It showed what we would do with the current level of public spending and what we would do with more money, covering housing, tourism, everything. We were specific down to the name of a miners' institute. I think it might have been a unique document. It presented party political problems for Labour, which could no longer say, at least with any conviction, that the commitments were vague and there was no new policy.

Newspapers, many of them Socialist in outlook, could see for the first time exactly what was going to happen, and they applauded.

The private sector was asked to help on particular projects. I went to the two largest breweries, Whitbreads and Welsh Breweries, a subsidiary of Bass, and said that if I was to clear up the valleys they should act, too. Both were considering action. I asked them to produce plans to show what they would do in the next three years. They gave me a commitment to spend nearly forty million pounds on cleaning up the pubs in the valleys. I asked the ten biggest industrialists for their capital programmes over the next three years.

It was not just a question of what the government was doing. Everyone saw that over three years the valleys were going to improve substantially. The gradual decline was to be halted.

What was exciting was that during the period I was in the Welsh Office, unemployment fell faster than in any other part of the United Kingdom. Unemployment in the valleys fell faster than in any other part of Wales. The leaders of the Labour councils knew it and praised it privately, but could not publicly for party political reasons . . .

The full Valleys Initiative covered the Welsh economy, education and training, tourism and the arts, roads, the environment, voluntary effort, health and social services and housing. The programme included:
* New schemes to assist small businesses
* Research projects to promote new opportunities for Welsh firms, such as developing the clothing industry and joint purchasing and marketing by small firms
* Export advice
* A new centre for Quality Enterprise and Design
* A Welsh Technology Development fund to help firms translate new ideas into sales
* Plans for the 3is, Investors in Industry, to invest at least £2.5 million in the valleys in a single year, two thirds more than in previous years
* A trebling of spending on an advanced factory and workshop programme
* A new campaign to improve the standard of retailing
* New links between business and schools in each valley

* A training commission to carry out a 'skills audit' and identify the skills likely to be needed by existing and potential employers
* A marketing scheme to attract more visitors to the valleys
* An enhanced road improvement programme
* UK2000 to promote more practical projects to improve the environment, provide training and create jobs
* Increased funding for the Prince of Wales Committee
* Funding of two valley health centres and twelve other projects, including a day hospital and community hospital
* Further capital allocations worth eight million pounds to improve housing stock . . .

When it came to enticing overseas investment, I looked closely at Japan. Japan had already established some factories in the Principality and Wales did have a good reputation. Japan would remain a prime target, but we wanted, too, to pull in firms from the United States and parts of Europe where it was in their interests to have manufacturing in Britain. I conducted a study of the international possibilities and set up a small group to manage the strategy, attracting high-calibre people like Sir John Harvey-Jones, the immediate past chairman of ICI, and Desmond Watkins, one of Shell's top men . . .

By the time I left Wales unemployment had been more than halved, from thirteen to six per cent, and was only one and a half per cent higher than in south-east England. It was the biggest drop in the United Kingdom.

(Peter Walker, *Staying Power: An Autobiography*, London, Bloomsbury, 1991, pp.207–9, 211.)

A.14 In the wake of the 1979 Referendum the prospects for constitutional change for Wales seem firmly linked to some measures being brought forward for decentralisation for Britain as a whole, or for England and Wales together if Scottish devolution, as seems likely, paves the way. Given the long background to the devolution debate in Wales, however, events might develop more quickly once there was some movement elsewhere in Britain.

Meanwhile, the pressure for development of institutions, the dynamic behind Welsh devolution, continues. Three examples which, in each case, have arisen out of real community needs, are sufficient to make the point. At regular intervals during the last 30 years action groups have formed to fight closure threats to Welsh railway lines. During 1982 both the Welsh Consumer Council and the Welsh Counties Committee called for a Transport Authority for Wales to plan and finance an integrated transport policy involving railways, roads and buses.

The second example concerns the growth of Welsh medium education, largely the result of parents coming together to assert their rights under the 1944 Education Act and force Welsh education authorities to set up Welsh medium schools. Between 1970 and 1984 the number of primary school children being taught through the medium of Welsh rose from 6,243 to 10,412, and secondary school children from 2,017 to 8,933. However, by the early 1980s Cymdeithas yr Iaith Gymraeg judged that the Welsh schools movement was losing momentum, because of financial cut-backs in education budgets and hostility on the part of some education authorities. So in 1983 it launched a new campaign to establish a Welsh Language Education Development Body to co-ordinate and promote a language strategy for Wales as a whole: 'There is a specific need, requiring a specific body with a specific finance budget.'

The third example arose spontaneously out of the long-drawn-out struggle of the Welsh miners to defend their pits and communities during the 1984–5 coal dispute. The network of Miners' Support Groups that grew up in all parts of Wales, not just the mining areas, during the dispute was co-ordinated by the Wales Congress in Support of Mining Communities. This was a significant initiative in that it brought together a broad coalition of Left-wing forces in Wales, including Plaid Cymru and Labour MPs who not only shared platforms, but the work of organising the campaign as well. Many viewed the Congress as a surrogate Welsh Assembly . . .

Yet history shows that the Welsh do seem to recoil instinctively whenever there is an opportunity to assert their national identity. It is as though Wales has lived too long in the shadow of a powerful English presence to risk brash adventure: much better to make progress quietly, by stealth. A reading of this book, however, should indicate that while such caution may have paid dividends in the past, the world is now changing beyond recognition. In the Wales of the 1980s more than a century of single-party politics is being transformed into a far more fluid multi-party system; the Labour Party seems on the slide in England; the British nation-state is being challenged in Brussels and Belfast; Scottish politics remain an uncertain but potentially influential focus for change; and, as has been described in this essay, a variety of institutional and administrative expressions of Welsh identity continue to evolve. We should not be too surprised if we wake up some time in the 1990s to find the kind of modest political arrangements envisaged in the 1978 Wales Act to be the most natural way to accommodate us to the changing patterns of the last part of the 20th Century.

(John Osmond, 'The Dynamic of Institutions' in John Osmond (ed.), *The National Question Again: Welsh Political Identity in the 1980s*, Llandysul, Gomer, 1985, pp.252–4.)

The Welsh Language

JANET DAVIES

'How long can it last?' asks the teacher in Ned Thomas's 'Six Characters in Search of Tomorrow'. It was hardly a new question. About 1600 the poet Edwart ap Raff complained that 'the world has gone all English', and that at a time when the overwhelming majority in Wales was monoglot Welsh, and a not inconsiderable number to the east of Offa's Dyke were Welsh speakers. There were others who took a more optimistic view. In 1885, for example, Dan Isaac Davies prophesied that there would be three million bilingual citizens in Wales by 1985. Speculation on the present and future state of the Welsh language is a continuing theme in Welsh history.

The census of 1951 recorded that 714,686 (28.9 per cent) of the people of Wales claimed to be able to speak Welsh. Almost all the areas containing a high percentage of Welsh speakers were rural. Welsh was no longer spoken over a solid, unbroken block of territory; instead, smaller Welsh-speaking areas were surrounded by areas of considerable anglicization. Adult monoglot Welsh speakers had virtually disappeared. The 1951 statistics were part of a progression which had begun with the first language census in 1891, and appeared to bear out the predictions of those who had for many years been prophesying the imminent demise of Welsh. The second half of the twentieth century, however, was to witness a number of significant developments. The number of Welsh speakers continued to decline, but their distribution, geographically and by age, changed, while other factors had their effect on the status of the language, and on perceptions of it.

Census returns revealed that 26 per cent (656,022) of the

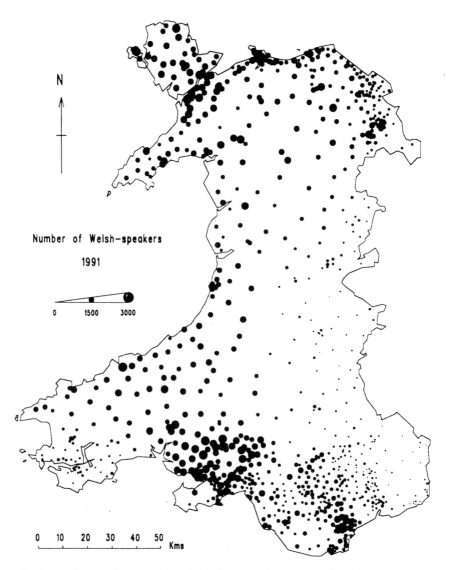

Number of Welsh speakers, 1991. (*Source: J. Aitchison and H. Carter,* A Geography of the Welsh Language 1969–1991, *1994.)*

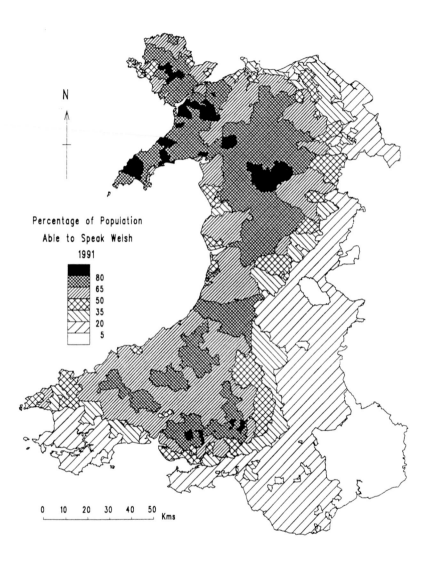

Percentage of the population able to speak Welsh, 1991. (*Source: J. Aitchison and H. Carter*, A
Geography of the Welsh Language 1969–1991, *1994.*)

people of Wales claimed to speak Welsh in 1961, 20.9 per cent (542,425) in 1971, 18.9 per cent (508,207) in 1981 and 18.6 per cent (508,098) in 1991. Employment opportunities were declining in those areas traditionally regarded as the heartland of the Welsh language. Quarrying in Arfon, coal-mining in eastern Carmarthenshire and western Glamorgan (the areas with the highest numbers of Welsh speakers) and, above all, agriculture had contracted, forcing many to move from their home areas. This development, in turn, led to a surplus of housing stock and an increase in in-migration. The population of many rural areas increased between 1961 and 1981, bolstered for the most part by incomers seeking an alternative to an urban lifestyle

B.1 (B.1). In many communities which had been Welsh-speaking for centuries, the linguistic pattern changed. By 1991, Gwynedd and Dyfed were still the main strongholds of the Welsh language, accounting for more than half of all Welsh speakers. High numbers of Welsh speakers were to be found in the industrial areas of east Carmarthenshire and west Glamorgan and also in Cardiff and its immediate hinterland. They were also to be found in towns: the towns of the northern and western coasts and many of the rural inland towns. Welsh, long associated with rural areas (despite its successful transplantation to the industrial areas in the nineteenth century) had become, in terms of absolute numbers and of density of speakers, an urban

B.2 and suburban language (B.2). In some urban districts it had been a majority language in the fairly recent past, but had not been passed from one generation to the next. This was the case in the borough of Merthyr Tydfil where, in 1971, 41 per cent of Welsh speakers came from the 15 per cent of the inhabitants aged over sixty-five. In other areas there was substantial in-migration from Welsh-speaking areas. This was particularly true of Cardiff; by 1991, 10 per cent of all Welsh speakers lived within twenty-five kilometres of the capital, and their numbers had increased from 9,623 in 1951 to 17,236 in 1991.

By 1991, the rate of decline among the numbers of those speaking Welsh had slowed markedly while, in one age group, numbers had actually increased. In 1981, 18 per cent of those aged between three and fifteen claimed to be able to speak Welsh; in 1991, the figure was 24.9. For the first time since the language census of 1891, knowledge of Welsh was more wide-spread among children than it was among the population as a whole. This phenomenon was more marked in the anglicized districts than it was in the Welsh-speaking areas. In Gwynedd, for example, 77.6 per cent of children aged between three and fifteen had a knowledge of Welsh, compared with 61 per cent of the population as a whole; in Clwyd, the percentages were 31.7 and 18.2.

Demographic change in Wales between 1951 and 1991 was therefore not merely a matter of overall numbers. Nor were demographic changes the only ones. The later twentieth century was to see an increased emphasis on the value and importance of minority languages — languages which are not the offical language of their state — throughout western Europe. In 1983 the European Bureau for Lesser-Used Languages was established to preserve and promote such languages, to raise their status in public life and to increase their use in the spheres of education, the media and local and regional government. Parallel developments were to take place in Wales.

In 1945 Welsh had virtually no public status. The Welsh Courts Act of 1942 had given Welsh speakers the right to use their language in courts of law only if they were in a position to argue that they would be disadvantaged if obliged to use B.3   English (B.3). Welsh was hardly ever to be seen on buildings (apart from Welsh chapels), on official forms or on public notices, nor was it used in post offices, by telephone operators B.4   or in conducting local government business (B.4). In 1952 two Llanelli residents, Eileen and Trefor Beasley, made a request for a bilingual rate-demand and received a peremptory refusal from Llanelli Rural District Council. The council eventually yielded eight years later.

In February 1962 Saunders Lewis delivered the BBC's annual lecture in Wales on the theme *Tynged yr Iaith* (The Fate of the B.5   Language) (B.5). In the summer of 1962 Cymdeithas yr Iaith Gymraeg (the Welsh Language Society) was founded to take up B.6   this challenge (B.6). A series of campaigns followed, for the use of Welsh on court summonses, in the post office, on car licences, on road-signs and in the registration of births.

Members of the society engaged in non-violent law-breaking in pursuit of equal status for the Welsh language, and their activities were viewed with tacit approval by large numbers of Welsh speakers (B.7). The Society conducted protests against the rise in the number of holiday homes and other developments which it considered were undermining the viability of Welsh-speaking communities. By the 1990s, it was advocating a wide range of policies on, among other things, housing, local government and education. It also took into account changes in the distribution pattern of Welsh — the break-up of many solidly Welsh-speaking districts and the increasing number of Welsh speakers living outside those districts — by putting forward the policy of normal community bilingualism, under which all information addressed to any community would automatically be bilingual.

Pressure from Cymdeithas yr Iaith, together with a generally increasing awareness of the value of Welsh, led to an enhancement in the status of the language. The Welsh Language Act of 1967 stated that Welsh should have equal validity with English in the eyes of the law, although English remained the language of record in the courts (B.8). Public bodies — the electricity, gas and water industries, the health and social security services and the university colleges — had by the 1980s embraced varying degrees of bilingualism, as had, to a limited extent, some commercial companies. Following the reorganization of local government in 1974, Gwynedd County Council adopted a bilingual policy, while the district of Dwyfor gave precedence to Welsh in all its spheres of activity. Other counties followed more or less tentatively in their steps, although Ogwr District Council in Mid Glamorgan stood out against any improvement in the status of Welsh.

Gwynedd's vigorous language policy gave rise to protests. Claims have been made that the stipulation that applicants for some council jobs should be able to speak Welsh contravenes the Race Relations Act. Employees in the private sector have alleged that they have been dismissed for speaking Welsh in the workplace. There have been confrontations between members of Cymdeithas yr Iaith and commercial companies over the display of bilingual notices. By the late 1980s there was a growing demand for a new Welsh Language Act.

B.7

B.8

B.9

The principle of equal validity enshrined in the Welsh Language Act of 1967 had proved, under pressure, to be an uncertain concept (B.9) and the increased prominence of Welsh in the public sphere called for a more exact definition of the position. Drafts of a new Welsh Language Act which would take into account all these developments had been drawn up by various bodies and, in December 1992, the Conservative government introduced a bill 'to promote and facilitate the use of the Welsh language in Wales, and in particular its use in the conduct of public business and the administration of justice on the basis of equality with English'. A statutory Welsh Language Board would replace the non-statutory one set up in 1988 to advise the secretary of state; the new board would have powers to insist that all public bodies in Wales should prepare plans giving details of the services they would provide in Welsh

B.10

(B.10). The bill, which became law in 1993, was widely considered to be inadequate. Welsh and English were to be treated on a basis of equality only where 'appropriate in all the circumstances and reasonably practicable'; the people of Wales, therefore, still did not have the right to choose to use Welsh or English as they wished. In addition, the powers of the secretary of state, who could veto any proposed plan, were considered too great, while those of the Language Board, which would be unable to sue a public body refusing to comply with its demands, were too few. Privatized monopolies were exempt from the bill's provisions, Welsh-speaking defendants had no right to have their cases heard by a Welsh-speaking jury and there was no mention of the right to Welsh-medium education. The Act has been passed too recently for the effect of its operations to be apparent as yet, but its provisions appear to leave wide scope for future contention.

The campaign to give Welsh some place in the state education system had begun in the nineteenth century, when it had obtained a rather precarious and grudging foothold. Efforts to improve the position continued and by the mid-twentieth century it was the chief language of instruction in primary schools in those areas where it was also the overwhelmingly dominant language. Elsewhere, the teaching of Welsh to monoglot English-speaking children varied from area to area,

B.11 and there was little provision for children from Welsh-speaking homes (B.11). Then, in 1947, the Carmarthenshire Education Committee authorized the opening of a Welsh-medium primary school at Llanelli, an option which had become possible under the provisions of the Education Act of 1944. (A private Welsh-medium school had been opened in Aberystwyth in 1939.) In the 1950s other counties, notably Flintshire and Glamorgan, followed Carmarthenshire's lead and by 1974 there were sixty-one designated Welsh primary schools in Wales, attended by 8,500 pupils. This rapid growth was accounted for by the fact that the schools, originally intended to cater for the needs of Welsh-speaking children in English-speaking areas,

B.12 attracted pupils from English-speaking families also (B.12). Welsh-medium nursery education expanded in conjunction with primary education, and when Mudiad Ysgolion Meithrin (the Welsh nursery schools movement) was established in 1971, there were already sixty-eight schools with 950 pupils; by 1992 there were 600 schools with 9,338 pupils.

The rise recorded in the census in the numbers of those aged between three and fifteen claiming to be able to speak Welsh is closely linked with the spread of Welsh-medium schools. In Cardiff, for example, where the original eighteen-pupil school established in 1949 had, by 1992, been replaced by six schools with a total of 1,400 pupils, the ability to speak Welsh was 153 per cent greater in the five to fifteen age group than it was among the population as a whole. Those attending Welsh-medium schools in overwhelmingly English-speaking areas, however, frequently lack opportunities to use the language

B.13 outside school (B.13), while the very existence of the schools may have aroused a certain degree of hostility towards the

B.14 Welsh language (B.14).

Hostility to Welsh-medium primary education has been more marked in the predominantly Welsh-speaking areas where instruction in most schools was given mainly through the medium of Welsh. The sharp rise in in-migration to rural areas created a difficult situation for teachers, who were faced with an increasing number of pupils unable to understand the language which these teachers had been accustomed to using in

B.15 the classroom (B.15). Accumulated pressures gave rise to a demand for designated Welsh-medium schools in those areas also. Attempts by local authorities to formulate policies to deal with the situation frequently provoked a hostile response. In Dyfed, for example, where schools were divided into categories, the predominance of Category A schools — those giving precedence to Welsh — throughout the rural areas other than south Pembrokeshire provoked an angry response from some parents who wished their children to be educated through the medium of English.

Only a small percentage of primary-school children in Wales attend Welsh-medium schools. The teaching of Welsh as a second language improved in the 1950s and 1960s, with the adoption of new teaching methods and attractive teaching materials. By 1990 about 75 per cent of primary-school pupils in Wales had at least some Welsh lessons, and the 1991 census results for Radnorshire, where 27.6 per cent of the three to fifteen age group claimed to speak Welsh in an area where the language died out in the eighteenth century, are an indicator (though possibly an over-optimistic one) of the success of second-language teaching (B.16).

B.16

The position of Welsh in secondary schools has also changed in the last half century. In 1956 the first bilingual secondary school, Ysgol Glan Clwyd, was opened in Flintshire. Most of these schools were bilingual rather than Welsh-medium, teaching science subjects through the medium of English. The Education Act of 1988 defined a bilingual school as one in which more than half the foundation subjects were available in Welsh; under the terms of that definition, there are now twenty-four bilingual secondary schools. The 1988 Act also laid down that in the new National Curriculum Welsh was to be a core subject in Welsh-medium schools and a foundation subject in non-Welsh-medium schools (B.17). Recently, however, following the Dearing Report on the National Curriculum, Welsh will not be compulsory in non-Welsh-medium schools for pupils aged over fourteen.

B.17

The use of Welsh in higher education and at university level has also expanded. About two dozen university lecturers, mostly in Arts departments, have special responsibility for teaching through the medium of Welsh, and in 1980 a Welsh-medium external degree was launched by the University College of Wales, Aberystwyth.

The 1950s saw the beginning of a period of change for the Welsh-language media. A wide range of new periodicals appeared, but potential readership was much more limited than it had been a century earlier, and production costs had risen. Welsh-language publishing became increasingly dependent on public subsidy, a development facilitated by the setting-up of the Welsh Books Council in 1961 and of the Welsh Arts Council in 1967. The growth of Welsh-medium education at school and university level created a demand for more books in Welsh. The Welsh poetic tradition, stretching back to Aneirin and Taliesin, adapted itself to the demands of the late twentieth century, and in the National Eisteddfod of 1993 the chair was awarded for an *awdl* on the Welsh rock scene. Novelists and playwrights have continued to write in Welsh, a number of presses have been established and there is a network of Welsh-language bookshops. A new and most successful development, and one which owes nothing to public subsidy, is the movement to publish *papurau bro*, or neighbourhood newspapers. The first of these voluntary, unpaid ventures, *Y Dinesydd*, appeared in Cardiff in 1973, and by 1992 there were fifty-two of them, with a combined circulation of about 75,000.

From 1953, the year in which the Broadcasting Council for Wales was established, there was constant pressure for more Welsh-language radio programmes, a development which aroused antagonism in many Welsh Home Service listeners who did not understand Welsh (B.18). The problem, in the case of radio, was solved by the decision to broadcast English and Welsh programmes on different wavelengths, a situation formalized by the creation of Radio Wales and Radio Cymru in the late 1970s. By that time, however, the question of Welsh-language radio had been largely upstaged by that of Welsh-language television.

Television programmes in Welsh were broadcast from the outset both by the BBC, which began transmitting in Wales in 1952, and by commercial television, which began in 1958. Since Welsh-language programmes were not understood by the majority of those able to receive them, they were transmitted at

B.18

off-peak hours, often late at night, a source of grievance to Welsh speakers. The fact that they were broadcast at all was a source of grievance to some English speakers (B.19). In areas where transmissions from England were available — in the north-east and the south-east, the most heavily populated parts of Wales — aerials were often aligned to receive them, so that many people in Wales avoided watching not only the Welsh-language but also the English-language transmissions from Wales. Welsh-language programmes represented less than 10 per cent of total output in Wales, and when a programme in Welsh was being broadcast on one channel, there was invariably one in English on the other. Nevertheless, by the late 1960s, broadcasting had become a divisive issue in Wales and a growing body of opinion, on both sides of the linguistic divide, had come to conclude that the answer was to be found in a Welsh-language television channel. Welsh speakers would be able to watch programmes at reasonable hours and English-language viewers would not have their viewing interrupted. Not everyone agreed that a Welsh-language channel was the answer. Some English speakers argued that there was no need for any Welsh-language programmes at all. Some Welsh speakers argued that potential viewers of Welsh programmes would be lost if all the programmes were on one separate channel. Another group emerged, and became increasingly vocal over the years, arguing for specific provision of English-language programmes made in Wales.

In 1973 the idea of a separate channel was endorsed at a national conference convened by the Lord Mayor of Cardiff. It received the support of the director-general of the BBC and, in 1974, of the Crawford Committee, whose report was accepted by the Labour government. The Conservatives committed themselves to the channel in their general election manifesto and were returned to power in May 1979; in September they announced that they would not be proceeding with the channel. There were angry reactions in Wales (B.20). Television licence fees were withheld, there were raids on transmitters and in May 1980 Gwynfor Evans announced that he would fast to death unless the government made good its original commitment. After a series of mass rallies, which gave rise to fears that

A march from St Asaph to Bangor calling for a Welsh-language television channel, 1971. (*Source: National Library of Wales.*)

the situation in Wales might deteriorate seriously, the government yielded. Sianel Pedwar Cymru (S4C) began broadcasting on 1 November 1982.

The last thirty years have been significant ones for the Welsh language. The number of those who speak it has declined, but it has made important advances among the younger age groups. Because of in-migration, there are fewer communities in which Welsh is the community language, but many of those who have moved into traditionally Welsh-speaking areas are well-disposed towards the language — nearly 10 per cent of Welsh speakers in 1991 were born outside Wales. Welsh-medium schools have attracted pupils from English-speaking homes, and there are increasing numbers of adult learners. The status of the language has improved — it is now seen as an advantage to be able to speak Welsh. This improved status, and the increased visibility of Welsh in education, the media and local government which go with it, have inevitably led to a certain amount of unfavourable reaction. Many factors, some of them beyond the control of those concerned for the future of Welsh, will have their effect on its development. None of them is likely to be more crucial than the necessity of convincing all who live in Wales that, as stated in the 1972 manifesto of Cymdeithas yr Iaith Gymraeg, 'If the Welsh language were to die . . . humanity would be impoverished in the sense that one thread among the thousands which make up the cultural pattern of mankind — whose glory is its variety — would be lost.'

Sources

B.1   For the Welsh language in-migration became a major issue. The reasons for this reversal have been widely analysed, and are commonly associated with the processes of rural retreating and counter-urbanization. The majority of incomers were those who were moved to reject urban lifestyles and who, with capital often gained from the sale of metropolitan property, were able to settle in more congenial environments, both physical and social. As was widely publicized, the influx also included other social groupings (hippies, drop-outs, artists etc.); less wealthy perhaps, but also in search of alternative life-styles. The critical point as far as the language was concerned, was that this in-migration was of sufficient order even to hide the continued out-migration of young people from the rural heartland.

(J. Aitchison and H. Carter, *A Geography of the Welsh Language, 1961–1991*, Cardiff, University of Wales Press, 1994, p.46.)

B.2   De-industrialization has led to significant population loss . . . the undermining of coalfield communities where if Welsh was no longer central it was still a distinctive element, especially in those areas of the anthracite coalfield where the largest numbers of Welsh speakers in Wales were to be found . . . agriculture was not able to sustain employment and it too saw a diminution of the labour-force . . . the administrative towns, such as Carmarthen or Mold, have experienced increases, if not within their boundaries then within their commuting areas . . . the proposed development at Cardiff Bay symbolizes the role and functions of the transactional city — administration, banking and finance, leisure, together with gentrification in the provision of housing. But in Wales, with the new attention to the language . . . facility in Welsh, if not an essential, is certainly seen as a great advantage . . . There has, therefore, been a clear migratory flow from rural Wales to the administrative towns . . .

(J. Aitchison and H. Carter, *A Geography of the Welsh Language 1961–1991*, Cardiff, University of Wales Press, 1994, p.47.)

B.3   Following agitation and a nation-wide petition . . . [the] Home Secretary presented a Bill to Parliament which became the Welsh Courts Act, 1942. This Act granted to 'any party or witness who considers that he would otherwise be at a disadvantage by reason of his natural language of communication being Welsh' the right to speak Welsh, and have it interpreted, in Court. The Act also purported to repeal section 17 of the Act of Union, but the habit of regarding English as the only official language of the Courts and officials had . . . become too ingrained to be much modified by an obscure Act of Parliament enacted in haste during a great world conflict . . .

English was still the official language. The 1942 Act restated that fact, by declaring that the record should, as hitherto, continue to be kept in English. Even as late as 1966, the then Lord Chief Justice could interpret the 1942 Act in such a way that *it was the Court, and not the individual party or witness*, who had the last word on whether a party or witness had sufficient knowledge of English to be required to speak that language in a court of law.

(R. Lewis, 'The Welsh Language and the Law', in Meic Stephens (ed.), *The Welsh Language Today*, Llandysul, Gomer, 1973, pp.196–7.)

B.4   It has always been a handicap for a small language not to be an official language, but never more so than during the second half of the Twentieth Century . . . when the state through its various guises speaks to us through so many servants, sends us so many letters and forms, displays so many notices and signs, teaches us so many new words and phrases . . .

By 1965, the process of gathering power in the hands of the state had been gathering force for over fifty years. Yet in that year the Hughes Parry Committee could report that, outside the field of education, the Welsh language had been 'in effect ignored by the British state machinery' and that English was the traditional language of legal and public administration throughout Wales.

(I. B. Rees, 'The Welsh Language in Government', in Meic Stephens (ed.), *The Welsh Language Today*, Llandysul, Gomer, 1973, p.211.)

B.5   Go to it in earnest and without wavering, to make it impossible to conduct local authority or central government business without the Welsh language. Insist on the rate demand being either in Welsh or bilingual. Give notice to the Postmaster General that annual licences will not be paid unless they are available in Welsh. Demand that all summonses to appear in court be in

Welsh. This is not a haphazard policy for isolated individuals
... It is a policy for a movement, and that movement should be
active in those areas where Welsh is an everyday spoken
language ... raising the Welsh language to be the main administrative medium of district and county ... To revive the Welsh
language in Wales is nothing less than a revolution. Success can
come only through revolutionary methods.

(Saunders Lewis, *Tynged yr Iaith* (The Fate of the Language),
trans. Elizabeth Edwards, in *Planet* 4, February/March 1971,
pp.26–7.)

B.6   It is not simply a matter of expressing dissatisfaction with
sporadic manifestations of unfairness to the language, it is not
merely a desire to have Welsh on an official form or a bilingual
roadsign, or 'more Welsh in the Post Office', which has moved
the Society to challenge the law of the land. If this were the
case, there would be some justice in the establishment's criticisms and the reproaches of politicians that the movement was
impatient of the normal processes of politics, and expected to
transform overnight a system established for centuries. If this is
all there was to it, if the Society were merely trying to alleviate
in some directions the injustices done to the language in 1536,
then the energy, the enthusiasm and the total dedication found
among its members would be ridiculously disproportionate to
the task in hand. But their motivation goes deeper. They are
driven by the realisation that the final crisis of the Welsh
language is at hand, that it could well be at the point of death
and that with it will die the national identity of Wales.

(Cynog Davies, 'Cymdeithas yr Iaith — the Manifesto', trans.
Harri Webb, in *Planet* 26/27, Winter 1974–5, p.80.)

B.7   In the late 1960s the campaigns of Cymdeithas yr Iaith became
increasingly militant — the Welsh version, perhaps, of the
unrest prevalent in those years among young people throughout the western world. The campaigns touched a raw nerve in
the life of Wales. Officials reacted with confused anger and
grudging concessions. Members of the older generation of

Welsh speakers were obliged to reconsider their allegiance to the language . . . Some Welsh magistrates showed sympathy for law-breaking; indeed, it could almost be claimed that they approved of it . . . the protest movement inspired an array of other activities — the Welsh pop scene, for example, and the efforts to establish bookshops, publishing houses, record companies and housing associations operating through the medium of Welsh.

(John Davies, *A History of Wales*, London, Allen Lane, 1993, p.650.)

B.8   . . . the Government set up the Hughes Parry Committee in 1963 'to clarify the legal status of the Welsh language and to consider whether any changes in the law ought to be made'. The Committee reported in 1965 that 'there should be a clear, positive, legislative declaration of general application to the effect that any act, writing or thing done in Welsh in Wales should have the like force as if it had been done in English'. This they called *The Principle of Equal Validity* . . . In consequence of this Report . . . Parliament enacted the Welsh Language Act of 1967.

(R. Lewis, 'The Welsh Language and the Law', in Meic Stephens (ed.), *The Welsh Language Today*, Llandysul, Gomer, 1973, pp.198–9.)

B.9   Time and again, a person who believes that a good citizen should use Welsh has to make a special point of asking for a Welsh version of a document, has to argue before the administration accept Welsh from him, sees, in Welsh-speaking areas, new English signs which could lawfully be bilingual. Even when Welsh is available, he is seldom positively encouraged to use it.

(I. B. Rees, 'The Welsh Language in Government', in Meic Stephens (ed.), *The Welsh Language Today*, Llandysul, Gomer, 1973, pp.214–15.)

B.10   . . . there is no single body responsible for discussing the future of the Welsh language and for ensuring ways in which the two languages of Wales can live side by side. The first step for the [Welsh Language] Board is to examine the situation in Wales today and to seek a vision of the kind of country that we will wish to live in.

(The Welsh Language Board, *The Welsh Language: A Strategy for the Future*, Cardiff, 1989, p.3, para.1.6.)

An Act to establish a Board having the function of promoting and facilitating the use of the Welsh language, to provide for the preparation by public bodies of schemes giving effect to the principle that in the conduct of public business and the administration of justice in Wales the English and Welsh languages should be treated on a basis of equality, to make further provision relating to the Welsh language, to repeal certain spent enactments relating to Wales and for connected purposes.

(*Welsh Language Act 1993*, London, HMSO, 1993, p.1.)

B.11   . . . we conceive it to be part of the work of the schools in Wales to relate the children to the two cultures that exist here side by side, however we may regard the relationship of those two cultures. This leads to the fundamental requirement that schools must teach the two languages. Having due regard, therefore, to the varied abilities and aptitudes of pupils, and the varied linguistic patterns in which, at present, they live, the children of the whole of Wales and Monmouthshire should be taught Welsh according to their ability to profit from such instruction.

(*The Place of English and Welsh in the Schools of Wales*, London, HMSO, 1952, p.100.)

B.12   One development stands out. This has been the growth in the number and popularity of what are generally called 'Welsh schools', but will be referred to in this report . . . as 'Welsh-medium schools'. These are schools in predominantly English-speaking areas in which arrangements have been made for the instruction of all or some pupils to be carried out substantially in the Welsh language . . . most of the schools in this category are at the primary level and are intended to meet the needs of children whose first language is Welsh. A large number of English-speaking children have also been admitted . . . at the request of their parents, and in some areas they outnumber those whose mother-tongue is Welsh. Nursery classes are attached to some of these primary schools, but in many places they are provided privately or are run voluntarily by parents. In some areas Welsh-medium secondary schools have also been established . . .

(The Council for Wales and Monmouthshire, *Report on the Welsh Language Today*, HMSO, London, 1963, p.101.)

B.13   . . . the language situation in Cardiff is critically poised. There must be doubt whether or not there is sufficient momentum for a sustained regeneration of the language . . . Outside very limited domains, indeed outside the school, the use of Welsh at home, at work and at play seems greatly constrained.

(J. Aitchison and H. Carter, *A Geography of the Welsh Language, 1961–1991*, Cardiff, University of Wales Press, 1994, p.86.)

B. 14   There has been a wave of support . . . from English-speakers, the heaviest demand for Welsh schools has come from English-speaking Glamorgan . . . On the other hand there has been a growing resentment, impatience and anger . . . an English-speaking working class, neglected and treated with shoddiness . . . [sees] bilingual language qualification shutting off areas of employment for their children. They perceive Welsh-language schools as nurseries of a new order of privileged beings . . .

(G. A. Williams, *When Was Wales?*, London, Penguin, 1985, p.293.)

B.15   The educational policy formulated [in Gwynedd] in 1975 made a difference between traditionally Welsh areas and less Welsh areas. In the former areas, Welsh was to be the main medium of instruction in Primary schools. When English speaking newcomers entered these schools or elected to attend designated Welsh schools in the more anglicized areas, an intensive course in Welsh was to be given so that they adjusted linguistically as soon as possible. In less Welsh areas, equal school time was to be allocated to the Welsh and English languages, and care was to be taken to ensure that suitable provision was made to safeguard and develop the mother tongue of the Welsh-speaking minorities in these areas . . . In early 1984, Gwynedd announced the launching of an experimental centre for immigrant children . . . Pupils who at age eight or nine, for example, enter a school where Welsh is the main medium of instruction, pose problems, not only for themselves, but also for teachers and for much curriculum activity. Gwynedd's policy is to give such pupils concentrated Welsh tuition for three months . . .

(C. Baker, *Aspects of Bilingualism in Wales*, Clevedon, Multilingual Matters, 1985, p.56.)

B.16   . . . an extensive zone where young Welsh-speakers consistently account for between 15 and 25 per cent of the Welsh-speaking population. By and large, this zone encompasses the main Welsh-speaking areas of rural Wales. Surrounding this core region is a patchwork fringe area where the proportions are generally of a higher order. Although absolute numbers are still small, the patterns draw attention to the significant impact of recent Welsh-language teaching initiatives in such areas as eastern Clwyd, the whole of Radnor, South Pembrokeshire, South Glamorgan, the Cardiff region, eastern parts of Mid Glamorgan and western Gwent. Here the percentages of young speakers frequently exceed 35; in many wards they are even over 45.

(J. Aitchison and H. Carter, *The Geography of the Welsh Language, 1961–1991*, Cardiff, University of Wales Press, 1994, p.105.)

B.17   Eleven secondary schools in Wales have asked [the] Secretary of State for Wales to exempt them from teaching compulsory Welsh to all pupils under the national curriculum.

The schools are in particularly anglicised parts of the Principality.

(*Western Mail*, 3 November 1989.)

It is easy to imagine the furore that would meet the request of a Welsh school in a predominantly Welsh area to opt out of compulsory English lessons . . . It is very often those who refuse to acknowledge the importance of Welsh in schools, that complain about jobs going to those who do speak Welsh.

(*Western Mail*, 9 November 1989.)

B.18   As regards sound broadcasting, the BBC said that it was the established policy to achieve in 'spoken word' broadcasts originating in Wales a roughly equal balance of English and Welsh . . . [It] added: 'To those who object that this is in defiance of the balance of English- and Welsh-speaking people in Wales, the reply is that the programmes originating in Wales are a relatively small part of the total programmes . . . which are available to listeners in Wales. To those who complain that a roughly equal balance of Welsh and English . . . represents a pitifully meagre weekly output of Welsh language programmes, it is possible to reply that this represents a fairer proportion of activity in the Welsh language than is reflected in comparable areas of activity in Wales.

(The Council for Wales and Monmouthshire, *Report on the Welsh Language Today*, HMSO, London, 1963, p.61.)

B.19   I have the misfortune to live in an area where the only television programmes available are BBC Wales, HTV Wales and BBC2. On the evening of April 10 I watched the final of the West Wales Rugby Union Challenge Cup. The commentary, needless to say, was in Welsh.

I am Welsh born and bred but, fortunately, do not speak the language. I consider myself as Welsh as any Welsh-speaker, yet I am subjected to streams of foreign language every evening on BBC Wales . . .

Filming the Welsh-language soap opera, *Pobol y Cwm*, 1993. (*Source: BBC Wales.*)

If the BBC is looking for ways to economise, I would suggest that BBC Wales should be closed down and the majority of Welshmen could then receive and watch television programmes they understand.

(*Western Mail*, 18 April 1980.)

B.20   We are concerned about the future of Welsh culture. We support the policy that all Welsh programmes should be transmitted on the fourth channel, since we feel that our culture could best be served in that way. Welsh speakers should be able to watch Welsh language programmes at peak viewing times, and not be forced to accept the inevitability of Welsh programmes being relegated to unsociable times. This means that using a single channel is the only means of securing a uniform pattern, full of Welsh language programmes . . . Television is an extremely strong communication medium, and care must be taken to ensure that it is used to strengthen and enrich the Welsh culture . . . The Government should be anxious to ensure that the wishes of the majority of the people of Wales are not ignored. Otherwise, Welsh speakers will be treated as second class citizens . . . even though they are supported by their fellow Welshmen who do not speak Welsh.

(Open letter to the Home Secretary from prominent Welsh people, June 1980, quoted in C. Baker, *Aspects of Bilingualism in Wales*, Clevedon, Multilingual Matters, 1985, p.125.)

Women in Post-War Wales

TERESA REES

The post-war period has been characterized by both major changes and continuities in the lives of women in Wales. Major shifts have resulted from women increasingly moving from the private sphere into the public arena. The growth of women's involvement in paid work has been substantial, but from a low base: female economic activity rates are only now nearing the United Kingdom average. The combination of equality legislation, increased awareness of social justice arguments and the activities of the women's movement have transformed some women's access to, and participation in, not simply paid employment, but public life more widely — local politics, the arts, voluntary organizations, trade unions and religious life. At the same time, there are continuities. Women remain invisible in some industrial sectors, in top jobs, on the boards of companies and among major public appointments and honours. Women continue to be the main deliverers of caring and domestic responsibilities in the home. And the aspirations of young women in Wales today, particularly working-class girls with few educational qualifications, remain truncated and circumscribed by expectations of a life that will be largely given over to looking after others, just like that of their mothers' generation.

This essay explores some of the changes and continuities in women's lives in Wales in the post-war period. It focuses on the inter-relationship between home and work, the private and the public. It illustrates the increasing diversity of women's lives and the contradictions they face as a climate of increased egalitarianism on the one hand intersects with rigidities in attitudes and behaviour at home and work on the other. It concludes by examining the increasing numbers of areas where women are addressing their own needs, in political action, employment and training.

Patterns of industrial restructuring in both rural and urban post-war Wales have had profound effects on family networks, working patterns and community life of both women and men. Some of the changes in Welsh rural life have been encapsulated in a detailed study of Cwmrheidol, a small rural community in Dyfed. Cwmrheidol has transformed from a relatively homogeneous, Welsh-speaking community (where men's and women's roles in the private and public spheres were recognizably traditional), to a heterogeneous collection of inhabitants now comprising, in addition to indigenous Welsh-speaking people (C.1), incomers — including Welsh-learning, middle-class English people escaping the rat race, regular summer visitors and tipi dwellers (C.2). Women's lives in the community are now highly diverse. All speak of 'not belonging' to the community — of being outsiders.

In industrial south Wales too, communities have become more fragmented: close-knit extended families have found it increasingly difficult to withstand the pressures of economic change and remain in close geographic proximity. While the image and stereotype of the role of the 'Welsh Mam' are highly contested, studies of Swansea in the 1960s documented a highly differentiated and traditional domestic division of labour (C.3), grown-up children remaining in the geographical vicinity ('keeping close'), and a sense of 'belonging' to a family wider than the immediate nuclear unit (C.4). However, while networks remain important in many aspects of social organization for many women in the 1990s, increased participation in paid work has altered the nature and range of those networks.

The tensions between balancing responsibilities at home and at work, and between managing both traditional and new roles are reflected in increasing contradictions and fragilities in personal identities. In the 1990s, women are increasingly negotiating a series of complex transitions in status, roles and reference groups. There are consequent dislocations in identity: for example for mature-age women students in rural north

C.1

C.2

C.3

C.4

Shopping in Canton, Cardiff. (*Source: Mary Giles.*)

C.5 Wales, as they are drawn back into education as the children grow up. Feelings of a growing sense of empowerment are mixed with guilt about neglecting the family (C.5). Women who never planned to have 'careers' but became further education lecturers almost by accident are now returning to college to get 'credentialized', to get the proper certificate to do the job. Demographic trends mean that there is a growing number of elderly women making the transition from independence to dependence, the strength of their networks with family and friends determining the pattern of that transition.

There are paradoxes faced by women seeking to establish identities and belonging across communities or reference groups which can be incompatible or even contradictory, such as Welsh nationalists who are also feminists, Welsh speakers who are also lesbians, Welsh businesswomen operating in a male network and culture, women seeking ordination in the Church in Wales, and Welsh women writers, poets and artists operating in an androcentric cultural milieu. These and other tensions and contradictions are experienced as part of everyday life for a diverse range of women.

Women and the Labour Market

During the Second World War, for many women the inter-relationship between life at home and at work took on a new dimension, with state-provided child care and strong moral encouragement, and even force at times, to work on the land and in munitions factories. Other families took in evacuees from English cities. After the war, of course, the role of women as a reserve army of labour was underlined when employers, state and unions colluded to exclude women from the work-force to ensure that there should be jobs for the returning troops.

Women's participation in the work-force has risen consider-ably during the post-war period from 29 per cent in the mid-1960s, to 36 per cent in 1971 and 48 per cent in 1992 (1966 sample census, 1971 census, 1992 Spring Quarter Labour Force Survey). Women now constitute 45 per cent of the Welsh work-force. Male employment has declined, meanwhile, to 69 per cent (1992 Spring Quarter Labour Force Survey), one of the lowest rates in the United Kingdom. Ill health in Wales is given as the cause of inactivity by many of the men, but this is also a factor among women, particularly in the Valleys, and women of all ages. However, many women in Wales are also involved in full-time caring responsibilities.

Part of the explanation for the continued rise in the proportion of women of working age in the labour-force lies in the pattern of industrial restructuring. From an economy dominated by coal and steel, and where women's contribution to agriculture remained largely invisible, Wales is now largely a service-sector economy, with much of the remaining manufacturing sector being dominated by women. The growth in the number of jobs in health, education and administration in the 1970s, particularly in south Wales, was highly significant for women's employment. Many of these jobs are part-time and relatively poorly paid. Indeed, in 1994, women working part-time made up a quarter of the Welsh work-force.

Despite the increase in women's economic activity, the Welsh work-force remains segregated by gender to an even greater degree than other parts of the United Kingdom. This segregation is both horizontal (women and men work in different industries) and vertical (women tend to be clustered in the relatively junior posts, in low-paid, low-skilled and part-time employment). Women constitute well over two-thirds of all employees in clerical and related, personal and protective services and sales jobs. In addition, they account for more than half those employed in associated professional and technical jobs, but in other groups they appear in very small numbers. Men, meanwhile, are more evenly spread across the occupational groups.

The political arithmetic of women in top jobs makes depressing reading. The Hansard Society Commission on Women at the Top (1990) bewailed the appalling figures for women in top jobs in the United Kingdom as a whole, but the situation in Wales is far worse. Overall, the public sector has a better record than the private sector and within the public sector, the Civil Service and some local authorities compare favourably with further and higher education and with the National Health

Service. The latter was severely criticized for failing to put into place equal opportunities policies. The proportion of Welsh secondary school headteachers who were women had declined to 6.9 per cent by the early nineties.

The relative exclusion of women from certain areas, and levels, of economic activity ensured that equality legislation of the 1970s, intended to diminish direct discrimination and inequalities in pay, would only have a marginal one-off effect. Figures showed that, in 1994, women in Wales still earned only 73 per cent of average male wages in Wales (New Earnings Survey) and that women's wages in Wales were significantly lower than those in England and Scotland.

This situation has its roots historically in the concept of the family wage, and the notion enshrined in the benefit system that married women would not form part of the work-force. In 1942, Sir William Beveridge, in his report on social insurance, was of the view that 'During marriage most women will not be gainfully employed' and:

> The attitude of the housewife to gainful employment outside the home is not and should not be the same as the single woman — she has other duties.

As a consequence of this, jobs clearly identified as 'women's work' have been rewarded in line with the notion that the wages attached to them constitute a second income. This ensures that for many women, even in the 1990s, their earnings can only ever be a component wage: they can only contribute to what an individual, family or household needs to live on. Such women will never earn enough to maintain themselves or their families independently. As a consequence, unless they can move into jobs which attract a 'family wage', by moving up the ladder or across into male-dominated craft jobs, they will necessarily be dependent, to a greater or lesser extent, upon either a man or the state or both.

The benefit system and employers' recruitment and work-organization patterns tend to be based on the assumption that a woman's primary role is in the home. Thus, women are social-ized into two adult roles, that of wife and mother and that of

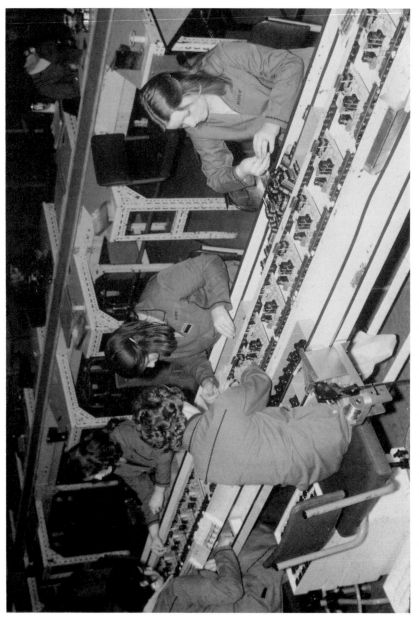

At work in the Sony Plant at Bridgend, 1975. (*Source: Sony Manufacturing UK.*)

worker, but the awareness of the one affects the other. A. Pollert's book *Girls, Wives, Factory Lives* (London, Macmillan, 1981), based on work in England, showed how young women whose jobs have been designed to consist of mindless repetitive tasks take on board the low esteem in which they are held by employers, and soon fantasize about the romance that will save

C.6 them from a life of factory toil (C.6).

The ambiguity in the role of women as workers in their own right is demonstrated by the checks and balances of the benefit system. When steelworkers were made redundant from Port Talbot, many of their wives, who had contributed to the household income through their part-time earnings, were forced to give up their part-time jobs because of the adverse effect that it

C.7 had upon the family's eligibility for state benefit (C.7). Similarly, during the 1984–5 miners' strike, if women earning part-time wages were deemed to be the bread-winners, then the family would lose out.

Women made redundant from a Valleys factory again illustrated the ambiguity of women as individual workers or appendages of men. Many described how they would not begin to look for another job if their husbands were unemployed as it was 'not their turn'. It would be difficult for the husbands to

C.8 'take' if the wives got jobs first (C.8).

The tension between these dual roles was underlined in the 1970s and 1980s when there were high rates of youth unemployment and increasing numbers of young single parents.

Single parents and Youth Unemployment

The 1990s have witnessed a growing moral panic about young single mothers. In 1993, the secretary of state for Wales, John Redwood, criticized a specific housing estate in Cardiff for its number of young single mothers living on benefit: an observation which foreshadowed the Conservative government's ill-fated 'back to basics' campaign. In other parts of Wales too, such as the Penrhys estate in the Rhondda Valley, teenage

C.9 motherhood is a common phenomenon (C.9). It is clear that in Penrhys, as in Ely in Cardiff, it is largely other women who are

C.10 supporting teenage mothers (C.10).

One of the main difficulties facing such young women, who are fulfilling the anticipated role of mother but not of wife or worker, is poverty. Child-care facilities in Wales compare badly with those of the United Kingdom as a whole, which, within the European Union, is second only to Portugal for poor provision. Such young women are increasingly in danger of becoming part of the problem which Jacques Delors, when president of the European Union, described as social exclusion. Social polarization between the employed and unemployed, the waged and unwaged, is a growing phenomenon demanding urgent attention. Beatrix Campbell explored the lives of young women and men in Ely after the riots of 1991, and concluded that while young unemployed single mothers were struggling to bring up their children, young men were struggling to assert their masculinity in the absence of one of its essential components, work. This had led, in her view, to alternative outlets for generating peer approval (C.11).

C.11

Young women clearly anticipate motherhood, whether or not they become single parents, and whether or not they find employment (C.12). Continuities were found between the generations in a study by J. Southall (unpublished M.Sc. Econ. thesis, University of Wales, 1990), which compared the hopes and aspirations of a group of Cardiff fifth-form leavers in the late 1980s with the experiences of women who had left the same school some twenty-five years previously. The kinds of lives followed by the women, of a series of jobs interspersed with childbearing and rearing, were remarkably similar to the lives the girls anticipated, although they were rather more hopeful about the help they would receive with child care than the experiences of their predecessors suggest were warranted.

C.12

A study of five hundred south Wales schoolgirls in the late 1980s found that decisions about the future were constrained by an anticipation of becoming a mother, in a way that limited aspirations for education and training (C.13).

C.13

Women in Business

Fostering the 'enterprise culture' has been a major plank in government policy in the 1980s and 1990s, and if the growth of the numbers of people in self-employment and small business is a measure of enterprise, then there has certainly been an increase. However, many people are 'pseudo self-employed' having been made redundant from reasonably well-paid jobs in the steel industry for example, and been bought back on short-term contracts. Many new businesses are low-cost-of-entry, low-skill enterprises which can undercut existing small firms through the subsidy of the Enterprise Allowance Scheme. Nevertheless, the self-employment sector is substantial in Wales. Unfortunately, women's contribution to family businesses, for example those run by families of Asian origin, is scarcely recorded or recognized, and women's own businesses rarely get the support needed from agencies, financial institutions or indeed members of their own families.

Many women are in effect 'married to the job', that is, they are expected to take a full role in activities to support their husband's occupation, profession or business, whether that be taking phone calls for a self-employed builder, or doing the books or feeding the calves and fetching parts for the tractor. Farmers' wives, who are likely to devote considerable hours to C.14 the business (C.14), had not been recognized as workers in their own right until a recent European Commission directive insisted that they should be eligible for the same employment rights and pensions as other workers. Even so, women farmers in Wales are often excluded from financial decisions by the banks who prefer to talk to their husbands.

A survey of women entrepreneurs in Wales revealed that gaining access to 'start-up' funds has been a major problem, and training for entrepreneurs is rarely appropriate, nor is child care provided. Partners will accommodate women's businesses as long as domestic services are not interrupted; hence many women run part-time businesses at home.

Self-help and Training Initiatives

Women have played an increasingly important role in public life in the post-war period, despite being largely excluded from decision-making hierarchies. This has often been the result of women setting up their own organizations and structures outside the mainstream to address their own needs.

Domestic violence has only relatively recently been recognized as a major social problem. Although this violence is associated with urban life, it is increasingly clear that violence in rural families in Wales is as prevalent, but often hidden. The women's refuge movement developed through volunteers and piecemeal funding: it remains dependent on donations and grant applications on a year-to-year basis (C.15).

C.15

The miners' strike of 1984–5 acted as a catalyst in that it challenged the role of women as essentially home-based. Women's support groups, motivated by the desire to maintain jobs in the local communities as well as jobs for members of the immediate family, brought many women into public speaking, travelling, representing their communities at venues away from the coalfield and even abroad. Many women were involved in food collection and distribution and other activities beyond their previous experiences (C.16).

C.16

As striking miners spent more time at home, women were available to attend meetings, participate in picket lines and so on. The experience of working in a women's group was to change many women's lives (C.17). While many women maintained that they would not be returning to the home, and that they had felt exhilarated by the struggle, despite the disappointment of the outcome, it is not clear that there were many opportunities for them to capitalize on newly discovered self-confidence.

C.17

Women-only training workshops have become a new focus for women working together in Wales, providing opportunities for other women who, with few qualifications and low confidence, would be unlikely to present themselves to mainstream training providers who do not target them or arrange training to suit their needs in the same way. The DOVE (Dulais Opportunity for Voluntary Enterprise) workshop in Banwen, located in renovated old National Coal Board buildings, trains women in traditional skills while their children are taken care of in an on-site nursery. The workshop has developed links with partners in other European Union member states and attracted

Miners' wives protesting against pit closures, *c*.1984. (*Source: Hazel Gillings/Tondu Photo Workshop.*)

European funding for developing exchanges and new training. From there, the concept of the University of the Valleys developed, allowing men and women of ex-mining communities to register for a degree at the University College of Swansea, while studying in their local communities.

Other initiatives have been developed by women for women, again often with European funding to develop training opportunities for women. The South Glamorgan Women's Workshop has recently celebrated ten years of providing training for disadvantaged women in a woman-friendly atmosphere: it has an on-site nursery, women tutors, is located near public transport routes, and has opening hours that fit school times and terms. Disabled women, those with no qualifications and women from ethnic minority groups in Cardiff are particularly targeted. Many of the practices, recognized as necessary to allow women with low incomes and poor basic qualifications to participate, are increasingly being emulated by mainstream providers, who now need to attract mature-age students in the light of declining numbers of young people.

Support for such bottom-up initiatives is coming from Chwarae Teg (Fair Play), and a unique inter-agency consortium of bodies such as the Welsh Development Agency, the Equal Opportunities Commission and the Training and Enterprise Councils which are concerned to improve opportunities for women in the work-force in Wales. Opportunity 2000, a Business in the Community initiative backed by the government, has thirty employers signed up in Wales who have committed themselves, exigencies of the recession notwithstanding, to improve the quality and quantity of women's participation in their work-force.

Such initiatives are clearly welcome, and are evidence of progress in the post-war period. However, it is clear that large scale cultural and organizational changes are needed, both at home and at work, if women's ambiguous relationship with paid employment is to be clarified, and if women are to have prospects of equal pay and financial independence. But there is no evidence of a change in men's willingness to take responsibility for domestic work, and, with women constituting only 3 per cent of the most senior civil servants, 3.5 per cent of principal local government officers, 2.3 per cent of company directors, 1.3 per cent of professors, 6.9 per cent of secondary school headteachers and 13.3 per cent of health service consultants, there is as yet little sign of equity at work in Wales.

Sources

C.1   We *need* incomers who have something to offer to the Welsh culture. They bring in fresh ideas and shake people out of their old-fashioned ways. There are some people in Ceredigion who never want anything to change. They think that you preserve things by putting them in a glass case to keep them safe from nasty outside influences. But there have always been outsiders coming into Wales and giving the Cymry Cymraeg a bit of a jolt forward. Or else people of Welsh family, like Saunders Lewis, who got a good grasp of European politics and literature before coming back and working for his own country . . .

   I'll help anybody who has something to give and is prepared to work hard. I'll have my young mothers practising Welsh so that they can use it with their children. I have read plays with a little group of learners before going to see them live on stage, and I like to help poor young teachers who are struggling with this new national curriculum, and some of them with only enough Welsh to keep one step ahead of their own class. Some learners do give up too easily, but others just don't get enough help from the Cymry Cymraeg. It's easy for the Welsh to go on about saving the language, but they soon get worried when they actually have to do anything with real live learners. They don't know what to talk to learners about, so they are embarrassed at being asked to help them practise the language. The learners don't know the ins and outs of a locality, or the ancient history of all the gossip, so they're handicapped in everyday conversation, and I've heard women in Merched y Wawr say, 'Well, what can we talk to them about?'

   If you want to save the language it's no use retreating into your burrow and criticising everybody else for not doing anything about it. I'm very unpopular with some people, because I've always been going around saying what I really think, but I don't mind being unpopular one bit. I must have been born with enough feeling of security to last me a lifetime, for it doesn't matter to me when people don't like what I do. I always ask for a Welsh speaker in shops or when I ring up the bank or Manweb. Sometimes it's a learner and then it's no use going on fifteen to the dozen at my usual speed (as some Cymry Cymraeg do, and expect the poor learner to understand the message). You'll destroy their confidence for ever that way, and it's all a question of confidence in the end . . .

Of course there are incomers who have no idea that they're coming to a different culture with its own history and language. They just think they're retiring to another picturesque bit of Britain where they've spent some pleasant holidays. Or they come to work here with a company, or set up their own factory because of the financial incentives, but they might as well still be living in Surrey or wherever it was they were living before. It's a terrible shock to people like that when they hear employees speaking Welsh, or their children come home from school speaking a language the parents cannot understand, or never thought existed. Because a lot of English think Welsh is some kind of English dialect. They don't realize it is the oldest language in Europe with its own literature going back to about the year 800 — about the time the English King Alfred was burning the cakes. If they've heard of the Welsh Princes like Owain Glyndŵr at all, it's only as rebels against England, or because they are mentioned by their own national bard Shakespeare . . .

(Quoted in Noragh Jones, *Living in Rural Wales*, Llandysul, Gomer, 1993, pp.338–9.)

C.2   While the men were doing the rounds outside, Lyn led me into the warm dusky interior of the bender for the first time, and put the kettle on the wood stove, to make tea. The whole atmosphere took my breath away. Outside the bender is not at all beautiful, because it is water-proofed with black polythene sheeting over the traditional tarpaulins. But going inside is like stepping back in time to some medieval nomad yurt. The frame is made of saplings curving in to the apex of the roof, forming a domed interior about five metres in diameter. Cross struts strengthen the wooden framework, and a stout central pole supports the whole.

The inside is cosily lined with old faded rugs and a few sheepskins. The sheepskins are a bonus, the result of Jan finding dead sheep which had been trapped in a barbed wire or other misadventure, too late to be rescued, too early to have rotted, and therefore in a moment of ethical nicety. On the way in you pass through a polythene porch on a slatted wooden frame with animal skull finials. This is where the boots and animal feeding bowls and water buckets are kept, and it also serves to keep the south westerlies out of the living space. The bender is heated by a stout old cylindrical iron stove, with a chimney pipe projecting up through the roof. This is also the means of cooking. A pot of stew can be kept hot close to the ash pan, while the kettle is boiling up on the top for tea.

The bender is all one circular space, but as one's eye gets accustomed to the candlelight and the stove glow, it's clear there are living, sleeping and kitchen subspaces. The kitchen corner is near the entrance. A row of spoons and ladles hangs from the curving wall, and little jars of home-dried herbs are tucked away above on part of the bender's inner frame of branches. There is a working bench of rough wood, and storage above the doorway for fresh food that has to be kept cool and as far as possible out of reach of Spit, the one greedy cat.

The sitting area is foam rubber slats covered with draperies, and there are more of these forming the sleeping accommodation, with a heap of blankets and quilts and spreads lying over them. Possessions (which are modest, since the whole point is to be non-consumerist) are stored in boxes against the curved walls, or hung from the branchwork of the bender's frame. There is a window of opaque white polythene giving just enough light to move around to find a place to sit, while more candles are being lit.

The air is scented with one of those bitter-sweet oriental incense sticks, perhaps sandalwood or patchouli. It is very peaceful and enveloping and womb-like, in spite of, or maybe because of the wealth of comfortable clutter, all with some useful purpose, crowded in a relatively small space. Every object is precious and has its own place in the internal logic of the bender, as we discover while drinking mugs of black tea. For this is our first visit and we are shown the treasures of the house. Lyn opens a flat tin box and passes it over. It is full of tiny vole skulls and rabbit skulls, the bleached remains of the black tomcat's hunting expeditions. From the same source come the finch's wing and the bright blue chest feathers of a jay that mocked once too often. Then comes a fox skull to examine, and a minute dried bat body of infinitesimal lightness and perfection. And oval stones from the stream worn smooth, and rough pieces of energising white quartz . . .

(Ibid., pp.198–9.)

C.3   The division of domestic work between adults in the home:

Almost all the daily houseworking is done by the wife/mother — the cooking, cleaning and tidying, washing and ironing, bedmaking, sewing and shopping. The husband/father in South Wales may make and tend the fire, and he will do occasional work like painting and decorating, some house-hold repairs, and car maintenance. Either husband or wife will look after the garden, though allotments, if taken on, are almost exclusively male preserves. In addition the husband may 'give his wife a hand' with the washing up, and he may drive her to the shops and carry home the purchases on a Saturday, particularly if she has a job. But men almost never take care of (i.e. feed or change) babies or small children within the house, though they may 'keep an eye' on them and take them out for walks.

   Among my informants, in families where the mother was dead, her housekeeping role had always been taken over by the eldest daughter living at home.

(D. Leonard, *Sex and Generation: A Study of Courtship and Weddings*, London, Tavistock, 1980, p.57.)

C.4   We of course encountered plenty of cases of quarrels, estrange-
ments, bitterness, hostility, and antagonism between relatives
within the extended families we examined in Swansea. But we
got a strong impression, confirmed by the statistics on proximity of residence and of frequency of contact and illustrated
briefly by the few cases that we have cited from the very large
number that might have been included, of the vitality and
meaningfulness of these sentiments of kinship. The extended
family may be a good deal smaller than it was formerly and
more scattered but the psychological responses to relationships
beyond the limited circle of the domestic group seemed strong
and important in the lives of the people we interviewed though
equally there was much idiosyncratic variation here from
person to person. Most people, however, and particularly
women, seemed interested in describing their relationships with
kin and in-laws as if they mattered, and clearly had a sense of
belonging to a 'family' wider than that made up of their spouse
and children.

(C. Rosser and C. Harris, *The Family and Social Change: A Study of
Family and Kinship in a South Wales Town*, London, Routledge,
1965, 2nd edition 1974, p.225.)

C.5   Underlying much of what they said was a sense of empowerment, in essence they perceived themselves differently. On
entering the student role they took on a new identity, which,
over the course of time led them to question the meaning they
attached to their other roles, and to a reappraisal of them. They
had developed a new, stronger sense of their own identity, as
separate from the family; they felt more competent and had
valid, informed opinions which deserved to be heard. They had
coped successfully with competing pressures and felt a sense of
achievement, but they were less tolerant of, and less affected
by, other people's negative attitudes toward them. They were
more sure of their own worth as individuals, they were
equipped to stand and fight their ground when necessary, be
this in the competition for employment or within the family.
These voices echo the sentiments of many of the women in this
study:

'I stood up for myself more, I realised my point of view was as important as anyone else's. I didn't take kindly to being put down, in that sense I did gain confidence. Relationships were better from my point of view, but it didn't go down well with my husband, he was used to me agreeing with him.'

'It has made me more confident and aware of myself and of him (husband), so that in itself can cause conflict. Things like, "Don't you talk to me like that", that sort of thing.'

(P. Garland, 'Educating Rhian: Experiences of mature women students', in J. Aaron, T. Rees, S. Betts and M. Vincentelli (eds.), *Our Sisters' Land: The Changing Identities of Women in Wales*, Cardiff, University of Wales Press, 1994, p.118–19.)

C.6   Mail Reception.

The quantity of incoming mail in each office meant that its reception generally occurred separately from its processing. In one office, mail arrived ready-sorted by post-codes and clerical staff were just required to check it off and transfer it to a conveyor belt to the rest of the building. Then clerical workers open and sort of check the mail. The procedure for this at one office until very recently was:

> The post opening section . . . had about 200 people in teams of about ten. In the middle there was a conveyor belt and you'd get an envelope . . . and you'd open it up, make sure everything was there, staple it together, date it with a receipt stamp, and it goes off and drops into this little box and goes on. You had people doing this all day.

Although that particular procedure has since been abandoned, partly because of the pressure and boredom experienced by workers, similar procedures were present in other offices. In one for example, a worker's sole task was to open envelopes and put them in the correct pigeon-hole above their desks.

It is clear that this kind of work offers very little individual autonomy or control over the labour process; the work came in a continuous flow, and any discretion extended only to the simple choice of the destination of the letter. The work must therefore be seen as essentially manual work; work which was also very routine and very boring. However workers had sometimes been granted some degree of autonomy, such as being able to get up and walk around or talk. As well as minimising the likelihood of any disruption, this also made working conditions more bearable.

(V. Winckler, 'Tertiarization and Feminisation at the Periphery: the Case of Wales', in H. Newby, J. Bujra, P. Littlewood, G. Rees, and T. Rees (eds.), *Restructuring Capital: Recession and Reorganisation in Industrial Society*, London, Macmillan, 1985, p.209.)

C.7   It was quite common to discover that in homes which had for some time depended on two incomes, both husband and wife lost their jobs in fairly quick succession, and we should remember the particular vulnerability of part-time (and therefore often female) workers in times of cut-backs and lay-offs. It was also the case in some homes that once the household came to be dependent on supplementary benefit the woman felt it no longer worth her while continuing in paid employment. Other women felt they should nevertheless keep their jobs, on the assumption that their husbands would eventually find work and that they themselves were by no means sure of finding another job should they leave their present one.

It is apparent from our research that the labour market participation of married women cannot be understood simply by reference to a rational decision-making model which examines the labour power available to the household and weighs the relative labour market strengths of household members. Although the notion of a household strategy is used by some authors in the discussion of contrasting divisions of labour in different households the rational-calculative connotations of the term take little account of the location of particular households within a local social network, a network whose influence is brought to bear both on beliefs about appropriate gender behaviour, and also on access to opportunities for employment.

Given a well-established pattern of female responsibility for domestic and child care tasks, a woman's paid work must either take account of her domestic obligations, or those obligations must accommodate her paid employment.

(L. Morris, 'The Household in the Labour Market', in C. C. Harris (ed.), *Redundancy and Recession*, Oxford, Blackwell, 1987, pp.135, 138.)

C.8   Some women did not perceive themselves as unemployed and so felt it was not legitimate to register. This rejection of the 'unemployed' label is probably associated with the blurring of the boundaries for women between employment and economic inactivity and between unemployment and economic activity which renders their classification in the labour market problematic. Other women did not want to adopt the 'unemployed' label associated with registering for work or did not want confirmation of their unemployed status. Some women did not register because they were discouraged from looking for paid work because of the poor state of the economy. Finally, the attitudes of some women illustrated the 'queuing principle', namely, that in times of high unemployment, certain social groups are felt to have greater claims to paid employment. In other words, some women defined themselves out of the labour market because they felt that they were unlikely to get paid work or because they believed that they had no right to paid work.

(C. Callender, 'Redundancy, Unemployment and Poverty', in G. Glendining and J. Millar (eds.), *Women and Poverty in Britain: 1990s*, London, Harvester Wheatsheaf, 1992, p.141.)

C.9   Penrhys was planned in the mid-1960s to prevent population leaching from the Rhondda to Llantrisant and the coastal belt. Unbelievably, looking back, there was also felt to be a need to provide high-quality housing to attract miners from Durham to the coalfield. With the valley floor crammed with housing, pit-heads, small factories, roads and railways, the only available space was on the hilltop.

    At the start Penrhys was regarded as a desirable place to live.

The houses were among the first in the Valleys to have central heating. Rents were relatively high. But soon the realities of living on an exposed mountain top with gale-force winds and driving rain a regular feature of life, set in. The miners from the north of England failed to materialize. A rapid turn-over in houses started to occur with a large number continually remaining empty. This meant that whenever there was a housing emergency elsewhere in the Rhondda, Penrhys became the last resort. Steadily the poorest families, and those with most problems, were funnelled into the estate.

Two years after it opened the council planted 30,000 trees to provide windbreaks and improve the environment. Within months most had gone, victim to drought, vandalism and the legendary roaming Valleys sheep. In the gloomy downstairs of the Community Hall the shopping centre was reduced to just two businesses, a co-op food store and the post office. The rest were boarded up.

In the 1970s the fabric of the buildings began to deteriorate. Roofs began to leak and even the walls of the houses, buffeted continuously by high winds, began to let in damp. The maisonette blocks were the worst. Their stairs and gangways became prey to graffitti, rubbish, vandalism, drug pushers and the stray dogs that are a constant feature of Valley life. Penrhys began to earn its reputation.

A third of the population changes every year, and the main ambition of many is simply to get off the estate. Despite this, Penrhys has evolved its own life-support system which rests on a stable core of residents, around 60 per cent of the population. These are largely made up of extended families of, usually, three generations, often living in houses very close to one another. Especially for the women it is this network of support that makes life bearable.

About 70 babies are born each year on Penrhys, most to teenage, single mothers. They survive because of family support and because, in the closed Penrhys world, theirs is the normal condition. Nevertheless it remains a condition that few could envy. Kay Towel, who is feeding and clothing five children by herself on benefits of £106 a week, said it was not safe for her children to go out and play. 'You can get attacked just going down the shop,' she said. 'An old lady had a firework thrown at her recently, and my little boy finds syringes lying around the place. These teenagers are bored. It's natural they're turning to drugs.'

(J. Osmond, 'Dignity from Despair: Developments at Penrhys', *Planet*, No. 102, 1994, pp.56–7.)

C.10   The lads got into trouble and the lasses got pregnant. The one was on the run, the other was trying to make relationships. The one was killing cars, the other was kissing a baby. According to a youth worker who had, himself, been one of the lads, their culture was about 'proving themselves by having bottle, being good drivers, getting into places, looking for fights all the time, being a bit crazier than everybody else, being able to get control of other people'.

Another community worker reckoned that 'by the time the lasses have kids the lads are twiddling their thumbs. They just walk away from it. I've seen it happen for years. They never take responsibility, and they start having relationships with younger lasses of thirteen or fifteen as if they want to extend their own childhood. Lasses are just bodies to be shagged. Then of course the lads get in trouble: they're racing around in cars, or doing odd 'jobs' to finance the booze or the drugs. The lasses have the bairns. The relationship with the lad has broken down, but the relationship with his mother will remain. It's amazing. The responsibility bypasses the son, who does nothing, but his mother will be helpful, passing on a cot, or some clothes. Often the lasses will still go to see his mother, and go round for Sunday dinner. You go into houses to meet the women and you just know that they are coping with *difficult people* — the men go underground. As they get older they don't even meet each other any more. They don't go out, they're these figures who you must not wake.'

(B. Campbell, *Goliath: Britain's Dangerous Places*, London, Methuen, 1993, p.201.)

C.11   Among unemployed men — so the argument goes — poverty produces an identity crisis; their unemployment leaves them without a role. Is it a wonder, we sigh, that they turn to crime? However, these conversations with men about riots and crime tell us a different story, one that shows how unemployment *reveals a mode of masculinity* whereas the commonsense notion has been that it *causes a crisis of masculinity.* We know that unemployment and poverty produce a human and economic crisis for both men and women, but that is perceived as an economic crisis for a woman and an identity crisis, a gender crisis, for a man. Yet the masculine trauma lies not so much with poverty as with its assignment to the world of women. Archetypal proletarian employment, no less than the City, the Church, Parliament or the police, has been characterized by sex segregation. Masculinity established its identity by enforcing difference, by the exclusion of women. Unemployment denies that difference its institutional framework. The social space men inhabit becomes solely local and domestic, and that is the space they share with women. Difference is reasserted in a refusal to cooperate in the creation of a democratic domesticity.

(Ibid., p.202.)

C.12　On comparing our material with Diana Leonard's study of courtship and marriage in Swansea in the 1960s, the difference is striking in some respects. *Then,* pre-marital sex appeared to be the exception, sons and daughters lived with their parents prior to marriage, cohabitation was unheard of, and marriage was inextricably bound up with the assumption of adulthood. Now, pre-marital sex is accepted, not only by young people but also by the majority of their parents, and many young people leave home at some time or another prior to marriage (37 per cent of our sample had at some time left home). Cohabitation is commonplace, if not yet the norm: in our sample, 92 per cent of the young people and 58 per cent of the parents thought that it was acceptable for young people to live together before marriage. For some of the young people we interviewed, marriage may be deferred. It is likely that, in reflection of these changes, marriage may have become less bound up with notions of adulthood.

Some of these changes reflect the grim aspect of unemployment and the changing gender division of the labour market. We have already discussed the consequences of these factors for courtship and marriage patterns. More to the point, perhaps, is the importance of social change with respect to women's consciousness: the redefinition of gender roles with respect to employment and the family, the control by young women of their own fertility, and, more generally, attitudes towards sexuality and its expression. This, of course, is not to paint a picture of a revolution in gender equality achieved, but simply to say that some changes have occurred.

(R. Jenkins and S. Hutson, 'Gender Relations, Family Relations and Long Term Youth Unemployment', in C. C. Harris (ed.), *Family, Economy and Community*, Cardiff, University of Wales Press, 1990, pp.113, 114.)

C.13   The 'fixed point' for so many working-class Valleys girls was the certainty that because they would become mothers, and would spend some years looking after the children, there was no need to think seriously about a career or training or qualifications. The sensible option was a job that allowed you to return to work part-time: by definition this would be a 'woman's job', and one that would be unlikely to demand qualifications. A second 'fixed point', clearly not unrelated to the first in either labour-market or family terms, was an assumption that they would be economically dependent upon a man. Wages were expected therefore to contribute to, rather than support, a family. A third assumption to emerge was that the girls would stay near home, close to the family of origin. All this clearly implies that such choices that are to be made are narrowly constrained by what local employers are offering in unskilled work to which employees can return part-time.

Girls' assumption about their future role in the family, and what that leaves over for participation in the labour market, clearly has an overwhelming effect not simply on what choices are made, but whether choices are effectively made at all. Initiatives that are designed to encourage girls into fields currently the reserve of men have tended to ignore the other side of the equation. There have been no initiatives on the same scale designed to encourage boys to take a more active role in child care. Unless patriarchal relations in the family as well as in the workplace are altered, girls' choices, particularly of those with no qualifications, will remain so constrained that asking them about their visions of their futures will continue to engender surprise.

(T. Rees, *Women and the Labour Market*, London, Routledge, 1992, pp.57, 58.)

C.14 The Working Day

The most striking feature of the farm wife's day is the sheer volume and variety of work:

> . . . up at six, breakfast for the family (six in all), do dishes and put laundry in machine to hang out later. Tidy and hoover downstairs and make sure father (in-law) is right for the morning. Answer phone three times before 9.00 a.m. — all to do with the farm. 'Ministry' arrived at 9.30 a.m. to scan 'Chernobyl' sheep — help husband drive and catch these. Finished at 2.30 p.m. — but make lunch for everyone in between and got washing on the line. Went food shopping (15 miles away) and called in at the vet's and farmers' co-op to pick things up for the farm. Did banking and called in at the accountants to sort out some business problems. Home, got dinner for everybody and washing off the line. Husband and son off to (rented) lowland to check stock there, so I fed the dogs (5), washed dishes and helped other children with homework. Did some ironing and went to village for carnival committee meeting (fundraising for community centre). Home around 10.30 p.m. supper for family and then did some work on accounts before bed at 12.00 midnight.

> (Mary Evans)

(S. Ashton, 'The Farmer needs a Wife: Farm Women in Wales', J. Aaron, T. Rees, S. Betts and M. Vincentelli (eds.), *Our Sisters'*

A Women's Aid refuge. (*Source: Mary Giles.*)

Land: The Changing Identities of Women in Wales, Cardiff, University of Wales Press, 1994, pp.124–5.)

C.15 In Wales there are 35 refuges for women and children escaping domestic violence. They are run by local Women's Aid groups. The existence of such refuges enables women who are being abused, physically, sexually or emotionally, or whose children are being abused, to escape from the situation and to decide, with support from the workers and other women in the refuge, what to do with their lives. Most women who seek shelter in a refuge have left home with nothing except what they crammed into a few carrier bags which they and their children could carry. Usually, they have been dependent on their partner for financial support, either through his wage or benefit payments. They have become homeless because the only way of escaping a violent domestic situation was by leaving the home they shared with him. As a result, they arrive in a refuge having lost everything and often in a highly vulnerable emotional state. Those running refuge groups provide support and advice to the women and their children, and if they are to stay in the refuge they help with the practical details of social security, applying to be re-housed, legal advice, schooling for their children and so on. Many seek refuge away from the area in which they have been living in order to minimise the likelihood of their partner finding out where they are. Large numbers seek refuge in Welsh refuges every year. According to Welsh Women's Aid's annual report for 1990–91, 1272 women and 1990 children stayed in refuges during that year and 6543 women sought advice and support from local groups.

(N. Charles, 'Funding of Welsh Women's Aid', *Planet,* No.96, 1992, p.85.)

C.16 The women's groups now became even more prominent, as they stiffened picket-line resistance — often in the face of hostility of the men. They also engaged in novel and imaginative forms of struggle, as at Cynheidre where they occupied the pit-head baths or in the Swansea valley where they sang hymns outside scabs' houses.

(H. Francis and G. Rees, 'No Surrender in the Valleys: The 1984–85 Miners' Strike in South Wales', *Llafur*, Vol.5, No.2, 1989, p.63.)

C.17   The idea of excluding men, and of restricting the groups to women-only, was a recent, and at times, strange phenomenon for the women involved. This is not to deny that single-sex leisure activities are a common feature of working-class society. Nevertheless, it was the challenge of feminist organizational principles which encouraged women-only activities, and which also forced many women to question their own role as women, both in political activity and community life. It also produced periods of friction, or open conflict, between Group members. To exclude men, and to maintain an independent stance in relation to them — and more specifically in relation to their once intimate political bed-fellows, the NUM (South Wales Area) — was still a new and at times uneasy experience.

(D. Adler, 'Struggling On', *Planet*, No.77, 1989, p.48.)

Popular Culture

PETER STEAD

In 1945 the people of Wales anticipated that economic recovery and the welfare state would generate a new social confidence which, in turn, would prompt a resurgence of a traditional and distinctive culture. Newly empowered Labour politicians were given to describing their mission as one of 'building a new Jerusalem' yet this was rarely conceived of as a leap in the dark. When Aneurin Bevan spoke of how he and his kind 'were the products of an industrial civilization' and of how their 'psychology corresponded to that fact' he was predicating a politics on the basis of what he took to be a general and well-developed sense of Welsh society. This was a generation that had experienced History: there were personal, family and collective memories of strikes, lock-outs, unemployment, neglect and then, more recently, the demands of total war. They were a people impatient to shrug off their disadvantaged condition and to commit themselves to a renewal and a flowering of those shared enthusiasms, many of which had originated in what was recalled as an earlier period of economic and social normalcy.

For all the talk of a 'new Jerusalem' the people of Wales did not live in a city but rather in a network of small towns and semi-urban villages which typically had developed for specific commercial or industrial purposes and which, to a quite remarkable degree, shared a uniform and unmistakably urban culture. The essence of that culture had been the mass participation of industrial workers, and to a lesser extent their families, in a full round of organized leisure-time activities. The pattern had been established in those two or three decades of

Salem Chapel, Winchestown, Nantyglo, on a visit to Aberystwyth on August Bank Holiday, 1952. (*Source: Welsh Industrial and Maritime Museum.*)

economic growth and high wages at the end of the nineteenth century and had achieved a frenetic crescendo in that last decade before the First World War. It was a culture in which strong support for the services of the religious denominations existed alongside an intense and highly competitive participation in musical and sporting events. Inevitably the ravages of the inter-war years saw that culture lose much of its brilliance, urgency and pride but nevertheless it had limped on. There were rearrangements, shifts of emphasis and even moments of real achievement. Wales had become more secular; there were fewer ministers and communicants, and increasingly those choirs, bands and amateur operatic and dramatic groups that survived or were newly constituted were run independently by committees. Wales also became more passive, with many opting for entertainment or solitary pastimes rather than active participation in organized activity. The cinema was the great passion of the period and there were many religious and political leaders who sensed that they had lost a generation to what they thought of as the largely mindless absorption of alien melodrama. Far more worrying was the fact that so many people rarely came out of their homes at all, and if they did so it was only to spend time in pubs, clubs and billiard saloons. Very few social leaders doubted that apathy was one of the Depression's greatest evils, and there was every hope that the renewed commitment to public life that the challenge of war had evinced would allow the Welsh once more to be enthusiastic.

Expectations were fulfilled and soon, in what was a new era of full employment and social security, the traditional culture of Wales was moving smoothly along familiar lines. It was, as in the past, quite distinctly a working-class culture, largely based on what manual workers did in their leisure hours. Not that people thought in exclusive class terms, for the rich pattern of recreation was entirely associated with a sense of local and Welsh community; and thus quite naturally the clerical, professional and business classes joined in and often helped lead popular activities. The sharpest social divide was that between those who had been to grammar school and those who had not, but that distinction counted for little in evening and weekend activity. Within communities there was a highly developed sense of the wholeness of the culture and its interconnectedness: individuals were rarely confronted with stark choices. Thus, in much of Wales, the culture was haphazardly and unselfconsciously bilingual: in homes, schools, pubs and chapels the tongues were mixed. Quite legitimately the historian may wish to distinguish religious and secular spheres of activity but, even in this respect, there was no dramatic *Kulturkampf*. As late as the 1950s there were family rows over the secular habits of the young and some churches launched a campaign to keep the Welsh sabbath holy, devoid of secular entertainment, but in general there was an accommodation. At the very least the vital socializing role of Sunday school and young people's fellowships was widely appreciated. Each community had its well-established calendar of public events and people were free to pick and choose their affiliations and their pleasures. Of course there was a hierarchy of respectability, with religion and choral music at the top, the pub and club at the bottom and with sport and the cinema firmly in the middle, but one vital clue to the culture was the way it nurtured and valued all-rounders. Young people who on Saturday had gone to the movies and then dancing might still go to chapel on Sunday and then during the week would make time for the choir, the band, a game of rugby and even a few hours of snooker.

Equally traditional was the competitive spirit, the need for the opportunity and rivalry to produce champions, and then for those champions to reflect and extol publicly the general sense of community. Success was shared, champions saluted. This was especially true of choral singing and team sports which played very similar roles and tended to run alongside each other. Many chapels and most villages had choirs, but male-voice singing was thought of as a Welsh speciality and in those post-war years the domestic supremacy of the choirs from Morriston and Treorchy was assumed to be an achievement of international significance (D.1). Glamorgan won the county cricket championship in 1948 but there was almost as much pleasure in the fact that in Gilbert Parkhouse they had developed a batsman as elegant as any in the land. At rugby Wales

D.1

won 'grand slams' in 1950 and 1952 (the first since 1911), defeated the New Zealand 'All Blacks' in 1953 and took great pride in Cliff Morgan, the world's greatest fly-half, as the 1955 British Lions' tour of South Africa proved. Cardiff City moved back into soccer's First Division in 1952 and regularly attracted 50,000 to Ninian Park. Even larger crowds turned up to see Wales, not least because of two Swansea-born players, John Charles, a regular choice for those World XIs picked by journalists, and Ivor Allchurch, the finest inside-forward in Britain. No wonder Wales did so well in the 1958 World Cup. All the while the medium of radio ensured that it was the boxers who had the largest following, notably British champions Eddie Thomas and Dai Dower.

It was a culture that had developed a quite natural celebratory and self-congratulatory style. There was no general awareness of the need for a cultural rethink; that was a matter generally left to experts. In fact, for several decades, Welsh social leaders had diagnosed the need for, and had been inaugurating, new organizations to counter the commercialization, secularization and anglicization of mass culture as well as the materialism of the Labour movement and the apathy of the young unemployed. With the return of economic growth and participatory enthusiasm the anxiety of social leaders receded but, meanwhile, two institutions had been established which would later assume major rather than minor influence. As yet the BBC tended only to reflect traditional Welsh culture and its main contribution was in exposing Wales to the cultural standards of London. The Third Programme played a vital role in broadening musical tastes in Wales but it was only *Welsh Rarebit*, a comedy show feeding off music-hall stereotypes, that tapped the nation's popular idiom. That circle of friends and contacts built up in the Depression by Dr Thomas Jones could claim to have played an honourable role in the way that the Arts Council emerged out of the experience of war and now its man in Wales, Huw Wheldon, could encourage and support the new Welsh National Opera Company and local festivals of the arts like that held at Swansea. But 'high culture', 'the arts' as understood in London and Paris, was still thought of as an occasional luxury, a supplement to the indigenous hectic routines.

In social terms education was a major priority and, strange as it may seem, that fact also precluded any need for cultural initiatives. Teachers had been identified as the country's greatest resource and it was widely assumed that, over and above getting pupils through examinations or to master necessary skills, they would inculcate a taste for the good things in life, not least music and sport. Everywhere grammar-school sixth formers were regarded as the favoured sons and daughters, but there remained the problem of all those pupils who left school at the age of fifteen, for they could not be expected to graduate automatically and immediately to membership of choirs and teams. The answer was school- or YMCA-based youth clubs which it was hoped would enjoy something of the enormous success of Urdd Gobaith Cymru (The Welsh League of Youth), which ever since the 1920s had been operating alongside the chapels in sustaining the cultural interests of Welsh speakers. These local authority youth clubs were to enjoy a particular success in running sports teams and, to a lesser extent, drama clubs (witness the career of Richard Burton), but they were only one strand in a routine in which the cinema and the dance-hall seemed more attractive options. Teachers and youth leaders were nevertheless crucial in this culture. It was they who nurtured talent only to see their most successful students migrate to England; meanwhile they played the vital role of ensuring that as many as possible of those youths who remained in the community retained their enthusiasms into their adult life. Activists became the responsibility of local committees and, in particular, of all those honorary secretaries, conductors and coaches who really ran the popular culture of Wales. As writers Gwyn Thomas and Alun Richards have memorably recorded, these locally elected officials were the glory and the bane of the culture. Many of them were merely content to guide and discipline popular enthusiasm; a minority, sensing the conservative and essentially amateur character of the culture, joined with adjudicators and academics in calling for a wider repertoire, higher standards and greater ambition. For the moment, familiarity and success coupled with the sheer popularity of that time-honoured calendar of local derbys, annual tours, eisteddfodau, quarterly meetings, *Messiah* and *Showboat* precluded reform.

Gareth Edwards, who played at half-back for Wales 1967–78. (*Source: Western Mail & Echo Ltd.*)

This culture continued to reward its activists and supporters and, courtesy of continuing economic prosperity, it seemingly achieved its greatest successes in the 1960s and 1970s. After 1964 Labour were back in power and prominent in the parliamentary party were a number of young politicians who seemed destined for the highest offices and who were quite clearly classic products of Welsh grammar school and village culture. Very similar types were at the forefront of a golden era for Welsh sport: Tony Lewis was the star of a Glamorgan team that twice defeated the Australians and secured a second county champion-

D.2
D.3
D.4

ship (D.2, D.3, D.4); and, inspired by Barry John, Gareth Edwards and Gerald Davies who were loved at home and admired throughout the world, Wales played its best rugby ever. In 1964 Swansea's soccer team almost made it to the Cup Final and, in 1971, at Ninian Park, Cardiff City beat Real Madrid 1-0 in front of 47,500 fans. There were still several very good Welsh boxers and one great one, Howard Winstone, who in 1968 gave a whole country the world championship which it had craved for half a century. All these things were collectively enjoyed and publicly recounted as were the exploits of Welsh superstars, especially those like film actors Stanley Baker and Richard Burton who had graduated from their local grammar schools and youth clubs to international stardom and prominence. In a manner that was quite untypical of people of their wealth and life-style they were proud to boast of the culture of which they were products and they made efforts to contribute to it. Stanley Baker's 1964 film *Zulu* was immediately adopted as a cult movie by the Welsh working class and, whilst the 1971 film of *Under Milk Wood* starring Richard Burton was not quite as popular, it was taken as further evidence of that star's credentials. In 1967 Burton had joined with broadcaster John Morgan and renowned opera star Geraint Evans in an attempt to ensure that HTV, the Welsh commercial television company, would sustain a high and distinctive cultural output. Little came of this initiative which nicely exemplified an era when it was assumed that great names could somehow guarantee a culture.

What had guaranteed and sustained traditional culture in Wales was primarily the dynamics of community and the tendency for distinction and success to accrue to that community

D.5   (D.5). Certainly, individuals were not under duress to make stark choices but what strikes the historian is the way in which, within the hierarchy of values adopted by most social leaders, the most respected musical and Welsh-language activities were closely associated with indigenous Nonconformity. Meanwhile, most secular entertainment was organized by entrepreneurs, and reflected predominantly English and, even more, American tastes and values. For several decades two very different agencies had organized genuinely popular and fulfilling activities but the structure of organization and division of responsibility had limited the range of options and maintained artificial boundaries. Those agencies were changing but not as rapidly as society itself. In the Wales of the 1950s new energies had developed, at first to challenge and annoy the existing cultural consensus and then, in subsequent decades, to create a new dispensation in which old distinctions faded as new opportunities emerged.

It was the dramatic arrival of a very different kind of youth culture which first began to suggest that a new era was in the making. For ten years or so after the war the youth of Wales had remained faithful to a fixed routine of youth clubs, dancehalls and movies, the style of which had been set by an older generation for whom the Depression and the war had been the greatest realities. 'Popular culture', Jeff Nuttall was to explain in his book *Bomb Culture* (1968), 'was, at that time, not ours. It was the province of the young adult . . . the culture of the jitterbug, of the snap-brim trilby.' What was desired was a new style and a new idiom and, as it happened, there was now money in young people's pockets to pay for the radios, the gramophones and the admission tickets that would effect the transformation. The turning-point in Wales came with the release in 1955 of the American film *Blackboard Jungle*, the opening credits of which were accompanied by Bill Haley and the Comets' rendition of

D.6
D.7   their 1954 song 'Rock Around the Clock' (D.6, D.7). In unprecedented scenes young people stood up and danced, some cinema seats were broken, the police were sent for. Wales had entered the modern era. There was more dancing in 1956 during the movie *Rock Around the Clock* and then in 1957, almost unbelievably, Bill Haley came to Cardiff for a gig. That

age of admiring Fred Astaire and Frank Sinatra from afar was over. The demand for rock'n'roll was insatiable and young people not only wanted to listen and dance to it, they wanted to play it too. All over Wales groups were formed, and one of the distinctive sounds of the era was that of drummers practising in front rooms and bedrooms. By any token Wales can claim that it was to make an honourable contribution to the new culture of popular music and rock'n'roll, and the standard histories do full justice to Tom Jones, Spencer Davies, Andy Fairweather-Low, Dave Edmunds, Terry Williams, Bonnie Tyler, Shakin' Stevens, John Cale and their respective groups. Their successes came in what was an international business centred mainly on London and New York, although the emergence in the 1970s of successful recording studios in Wales itself was an indication

D.8   that new domestic entrepreneurial energies were stirring (D.8). At first the new popular music might have seemed but a passing fashion, and one manipulated from afar, but in fact it was serving to change Wales quite fundamentally. More than any other agency it was the new music that indicated that there was much untapped energy, extensive dissatisfaction with tradition and the potential not only for self-expression but even for a degree of self-sufficiency.

At the same time Wales had developed a new politics. Most voters and commentators thought in terms of the Tory/Labour option but, from the late 1950s on, it was the young supporters of Plaid Cymru who were changing the nature of Wales. Their demonstrations against the planned flooding of a valley at Tryweryn in 1958 was the prelude to a new era of confrontation in which the Welsh language became the most contentious issue. The vital developments were the formation of Cymdeithas yr Iaith Gymraeg (The Welsh Language Society) in 1963, the direct-action tactics deployed in the fight for Welsh to be given official status, and a spate of parliamentary by-elections in the mid-1960s which frightened the two main parties into a recognition that they were in real danger of losing Wales completely. This was an era of world-wide student demonstrations and of demands for increased participation. In Wales, the only people who really breathed in the spirit of the time were those products of Welsh-language schools and Urdd

Gobaith Cymru who were essentially demanding the right to sustain a full culture in the language in which they had been reared. Their contemporaries saw them as an unreasonable political pressure group who were breaking the rules of consensus politics. We can see now that their protest movement was essentially of cultural significance: their aim was a more effective harnessing of energies within Wales itself. Prompted by a sense of crisis and opportunity, this new cohort of young Welsh speakers proceeded to adapt their existing traditions to the new era of rock, folk music and satire. Then, as their political demands focused on the possible extension of Welsh broadcasting, it was realized that what had been rehearsed at summer camps and at youth and fringe eisteddfodau was capable of being developed into a full television service. At one time the Welsh-language culture had been almost totally controlled by the chapels; after 1945, it had passed into the hands of schoolteachers and now, after 1960, it was the pupils of those teachers who took up a political challenge and in so doing came to realize the extent of their talent and the degree of self-sufficiency that was possible. A frightened London saw little danger in granting cultural concessions and so Welsh speakers were able very effectively to take control of their capital city and to unleash a new era in which young people once destined to be teachers could now be producers, directors, designers and presenters in a new Welsh television and film industry. It was a breathtaking coup and one barely understood by most citizens in Wales let alone the United Kingdom.

Welsh militants had seized the day and then the spoils. They had done so at a time when the old working-class communities of Wales, with their traditional culture, were essentially collapsing. First came the demise of Nonconformity, killed off essentially by television and the family motor car. Then came the closure of the pits and the other industries that had sustained specific towns and villages. At the same time, cinemas, theatres and other places of entertainment were closing and public transport was also being cut back. The passive acceptance of such changes can only be explained by the apparent inevitability of it all. Certainly, industrial Wales seemed resigned to its fate as compared with the way in which young

Chairing the Bard at the 1991 National Eisteddfod at Mold. *(Source: Wales Tourist Board.)*

Welsh nationalists had fought their corner. But there did emerge a culture of deindustrialization: historians, playwrights, novelists, poets and film directors overcame their nostalgia and called for a new pride in the Valleys as they took advantage of the new broadcasting and film-making structures their Welsh-speaking colleagues were creating (D.9). One of the most dynamic strands in this respect was provided by women. The miners' strike of 1984–5 had shown that women were as capable as men of defending the Valleys and, inspired by that experience, a new generation of Welsh women writers, academics, social workers and film makers burst on to the scene.

D.9

That process of historical transformation which eliminated Welsh industry and undermined so many local communities continues to astonish. Inevitably, a century-old culture died a death, but it did so just as a new generation was rechannelling its energies. The schools, largely comprehensive since the 1960s, remain the most vital agent, all the more crucial now that there are so few jobs for those who terminate their studies at the age of sixteen or eighteen. More than ever before there is a premium on individual success and there are contrasting fortunes for pupils who leave without qualifications compared with those who develop academic, musical, artistic, sporting and, increasingly, broadcasting skills. It is still a society that craves heroes but, although collective pride remains a potent force, the heroes and champions of today are seen as highly talented individuals rather than as a personification of community. Stars in the conventional mould, such as actor Sir Anthony Hopkins and opera singer Bryn Terfel, share the headlines with great athletes like Ryan Giggs, Colin Jackson, Nigel Walker and Steve Robinson, all products of black immigrant families. At every level there is an awareness that the realities of post-industrial society are pretty stark, and newspapers that proudly report the academic, cultural and sporting successes of local men and women also bear testimony to the hardships, tragedies and misdemeanours of those who still live in the shells of old communities.

The great bonus in the post-industrial culture of Wales is its capital city. Until the 1950s Cardiff was only an unofficial capital and in fact played no great political or cultural role in the affairs of the principality. Its emergence as an administrative centre has corresponded with its rise as a major venue for international sporting events, for television and film production, for arts festivals and for musical and operatic performances. The sophistication of Cardiff allows Wales to keep much of its talent. The country ends the twentieth century with a thoroughly distinguished, secular, bilingual culture, one in which Welsh speakers have forced the pace and applied the right pressures, but which allows enormous opportunities for anyone who chooses to work in Wales. There is much to celebrate, but two questions remain unresolved. Is this a culture whose logic will lead ultimately to a measure of political independence? And is it one that accepts any responsibility for all those people in the towns and villages of Wales who are unable to claim that they have never had it so good and whose popular culture is largely determined by the producers of English television and American videos?

Sources

On the occasion of its 50th anniversary in 1985, the Morriston Orpheus Choir (Côr Meibion Orpheus Treforys) invited the television journalist John Morgan to contribute to a Souvenir Brochure. Under its conductor Ivor E. Sims the Choir had established its reputation by winning first place at National Eisteddfodau in 1946, 1947, 1948 and 1949:

D.1

MEMORIES

Such excitement, and such cheering on those late nights in August in the Forties as we welcomed the heroes at the Cross, back from the victories at the Eisteddfod. With my grandparents and one brother I'd set off down Martin Street and along Woodfield Street with what must have been most of the population of the town. It's true there had been some dissension at 9 Plas-y-Coed where so many of us lived in so small a house. My grandfather William Sayce was firm for the Orpheus. But would his son, my Uncle Stan, my mother's brother, transfer to

A male-voice choir competing at the National Eisteddfod in the 1970s. (*Source: Wales Tourist Board.*)

the United? My mother, having been a life-long friend of Ivor Sims, believed only in the Orpheus. Even as a child I would follow the discussions with a curiosity that was to become an obsession. Strangely, it did not occur to me as at all peculiar that the two best choirs in Wales — which was itself the best country for choirs — should exist in the very same small community in which we lived, that our own household even should debate which choir we should support. Such easy familiarity with the best is a handy lesson for a child. Briefly I was tempted by the United, partly because they always kept on coming second to the Orpheus at the National. This may have been a natural sympathy for the underdog. I went to United rehearsals in the Horeb school room. My grandfather died in 1945 and men from both choirs sang at his grave in Llangyfelach, an experience as moving as any I can recall. I realized, though, that the Orpheus really was the choir to be near, even though they were the most successful. They were the most powerful and made the loveliest of tenor sounds. Ivor Sims would always insist the choir was ahead of the note, and would permit no self-indulgence. He allowed me to take part in the famous recording of Y Delyn Aur at Siloh in, I think, 1947, even though I had briefly been disloyal and was not truly fit to be a member of that memorable choir. But I had cheered the Orpheus with thousands of others on Morriston Cross on those famous nights; and cheer still. Happy Birthday.

(John Morgan, Morriston Orpheus Golden Jubilee Brochure, 1985.)

1964 ushered in what seemed to be a golden era for many traditional Welsh activities. The mood was set in Swansea during an August week that was in the main gloriously sunny: a very successful National Eisteddfod was held in Singleton Park whilst a mile away the Glamorgan cricket team were beating the Australians. Eisteddfod compère, broadcaster Alun Williams, did his best to link the two events, combining his introductions in the eisteddfod pavilion with the latest cricket score. The *Western Mail* caught the mood:

D.2   SWANSEA READY WITH A BIG WELCOME

Concert Opens Town's Second Eisteddfod

Swansea's second National Eisteddfod in 38 years opened with a male voice concert last night as Welshmen from all parts of the world poured into the town by road, rail and air.

Red dragons and three-feather motifs flashed a welcome to the visitors along the flag-festooned approaches to Singleton Park . . .

The Australian and Glamorgan cricket teams were welcomed by the concert compere, Mr Alun Williams, who told more than 7,000 people, 'I am going to speak English tonight because I want to welcome the teams. The all-Welsh rule does not come into force strictly speaking until tomorrow.'

(*Western Mail*, 3 August 1964.)

D.3   YMLAEN MORGANNWG

Ymlaen Morgannwg — this was your finest cricketing hour! The Australians have been beaten by the Welsh county at long last after 43 years of tremendous and unsuccessful endeavour. Never has a victory been more deserved; never has such an exciting and hard-fought match been played before in Wales; and never have 11 cricketing heroes been more deserving of their triumph.

The fantastic scenes that highlighted the end of this match at four p.m. yesterday at the historic St Helen's ground, when the last Australian wicket fell to give Glamorgan victory by 36 runs, will never be forgotten by the 7,000 fortunate and excited spectators.

As Hawke's wicket fell the overjoyed Glamorgan players grabbed the stumps and attempted to beat the invading crowd that surged across the ground in a race to the pavilion, but the jubilant spectators were not to be denied their moment of approbation, and swiftly they cut off the players' retreat.

The Welsh cricketing heroes were mobbed, and police officers had to rescue and guide them through to the foot of the pavilion steps. Once there Wheatley, the triumphant leader, waited and allowed his spinning heroes, Pressdee and Shepherd, to lead the victory march up the steps of honour.

What a moment of triumph for Wales; for Glamorgan; and for its 'adopted son' Wheatley and the two men of Gower, Pressdee and Shepherd.

(J.B.G. Thomas, *Western Mail*, 5 August 1964).

D.4   THE MAGNIFICENT ELEVEN DO IT BY 36
        WONDERFUL RUNS

A few minutes before four o'clock yesterday the small boys waiting on the boundary swarmed across the St Helen's cricket ground at Swansea. Glamorgan had defeated the Australians for the first time in their history — by 36 runs — and had become the first side to beat the visitors in their 1964 tour. The crowd gathered round the pavilion and solemnly sang the national anthem in thanks for a great victory.

(John Moorehead, ibid.)

D.5   LAND OF SONG AND INSTRUMENTS

With the Eisteddfod pavilion deserted of all but electricians ripping out the Press room telephones, and the 'battlefield' outside a mudbath scattered with the remains of sandwiches, it is the adjudicators who can best sum up the past week.

Hundreds of men, women and children have nervously climbed to the pavilion stage. For some it's meant the sweet taste of success — for others a nightmarish moment when they broke down, or forgot their words.

The sun blazed, the rain came down, thousands poured through the gates, and inside the great green pavilion the cheery adjudicators sporting their ribboned badges have been miniature gods.

The choirs of Wales are still the greatest, but the Principality is slowly becoming a land of instruments as well as song.

Mr Elfed Morgan, former music director of Carmarthen, said, 'There has been a tremendous increase on the instrumental side. Our object is to balance out vocal and instrumental music in Wales.'

And Mr Kenneth Bowen said, 'The potential in Wales is quite incredible and the standard is high.'

Mr Peter Gelhorn, director and conductor of the BBC chorus and former Glyndebourne conductor, told me, 'I have been very impressed with the professional approach of the choirs.'

But there was criticism from Mr Ieuan Rees-Davies, professor at Trinity College of Music, London, and conductor Meredith Davies, on the interpretation of soloists.

'The singers concentrate so much on producing lovely sounds that they often forget about the words and the meaning of the music,' said Mr Rees-Davies.

And Mr Meredith Davies added, 'I was surprised not to hear more uninhibited expression.'

The Eisteddfod ground at Singleton Park has been a world in itself. A crazy yet exciting affair for the non-Welsh speakers, an emotional, sentimental home-coming for the exiles, and a week of weeks for the rest.

(*Western Mail*, 10 August 1964).

The American Bill Haley (1925–1981) was the real pioneer of rock'n'roll and of the new fan phenomenon. His 1957 British tour brought him to Cardiff:

D.6   ROCK'N'ROLLERS QUEUE AROUND THE CLOCK

Requests from about 60,000 fans have flooded into Cardiff this week for seats at Bill Haley's two-and-a-half hour show of concentrated rock'n'roll.

Thousands of people, mostly teenagers, formed a queue more than a quarter-of-a-mile long yesterday morning outside the Capitol Theatre where the two performances of the show are to be held on February 21st. Some had stayed up all night.

Mr D. Ernest, manager of a music and record shop in Churchill Way, saw the queue and put on rock'n'roll records. The effect was magical. The queue burst into movement and before you could say 'Rock Around the Clock' people were rolling.

The Capitol Theatre and Cinema, Cardiff, 1956. (*Source: Welsh Industrial and Maritime Museum.*)

Postmen carried seven heavy bags of mail into the theatre yesterday. There were letters from Leamington, North Devon, Hereford, West Wales, Cardigan and thousands from Bristol and Cardiff clamouring for tickets. 'Phone lines buzzed with requests.

Mr W. A. C. Hall, the theatre manager, said, 'I have been in the business for more than 20 years, but I have never seen anything like this.' Last night Mr Hall said that there were only a few top price tickets left for the first performance.

(*Western Mail*, 19 January 1957).

Tom Jones, born in Pontypridd in 1940, has been one of the most famous and successful pop singers in the world since the 1960s. From a conventional rock'n'roll background he developed into a singer of standards and like Shirley Bassey (born in Cardiff in 1937) was constantly in demand in the world's most glamorous nightspots, not least in Las Vegas. His early career is recalled by a former colleague, Chris Slade:

D.7   THERE'S NOTHING BIG-TIME ABOUT OUR TOM

I looked at the name Tom Jones at no.2 in the New Musical Express Chart this week and I suddenly remembered my dad coming home from a club in Pontypridd one night about six years ago. 'Son', he said, 'I saw a young singer tonight who could knock that Tommy Steele into a cocked hat. Name of Tommy Woodward he was. And you should have heard him playing his guitar — marvellous!'

This Tommy Woodward had just joined my dad's concert party. Dad did tap dancing but the concert party also had an operatic tenor and a comedian. Tommy was for the young folks. I remember thinking, 'This singer might be OK but I'll bet he's not as good as Tommy Steele.' Anyway I got to hear a lot about this Tommy Woodward after that. He lived in Laura Street in Treforest, not far from us, and I used to knock about with some lads who lived next door to him. After a while he joined a local group, the Senators, and changed his name to Tommy Scott. Quite a celebrity he was becoming. In fact all over South Wales I would say that Tommy Scott and the

Senators became the biggest local attraction there was. Everybody used to shout, 'When you goin' to London, lads? When you going to show them Beatles a thing or two?'

Tom Jones — I mean Tommy Scott! — had been with the Senators a little while when I joined as a drummer. I used to work in a shoe shop in Treforest and after I heard the vacancy was going they auditioned me in a local pub called the Thorn Hotel. We had some marvellous times, Tom and I and the rest of the group. He's a great guy with a marvellously earthy sense of humour — in fact Tom's sense of humour helped us through some of the hard times before Unusual made the charts.

I remember when we first came back to London to record, for Joe Meek it was. We were excited out of our minds about that. We really thought we'd made it. We travelled down in the van and we spent a day recording (Joe had been introduced to us by some managers we had then, Myron and Byron. Don't ask me their full names — they never told us!) Two months just went by after that, but no record was released. Tom was dead choked and he was not the only one. After that we more or less just did gigs in South Wales and got to think we'd probably never be famous.

When we came back to London our new manager, Gordon Mills, used to give us £1 a day each to live on. I don't know what we would have done without Gordon — he gave Tom and us our break and he more or less looked after us for about a year before It's not Unusual. Nearly £2000 Gordon paid out . . .

Tom is still the same he ever was — the only thing that's changed is the Rolls and the cigar. But what's wrong with those especially when you can afford them? He certainly has not become flash or big-time since getting hit records . . . One thing that just hasn't changed is his determination to sing the kind of songs he really feels. In the old days he used to have his side-burns and wear tight leathers, but he didn't want to sing just the pop songs like the other local groups!

(Chris Slade talking to Alan Smith, *New Musical Express*, 19 August 1967.)

The keyboard player John Cale was born in Wales in 1940. He came to fame with the New York avant-garde rock band The Velvet Underground. In recent years he has given several concerts in Wales:

D.8   ECHOES OF THE UNDERGROUND

'What's it all about then, John, your song A Child's Christmas in Wales? One of your more enigmatic numbers?'

Twenty years or more after buying John Cale's classic *Paris 1919* album here at last was a chance to find out — from the man himself.

John Cale, born March 9, 1942, in Garnant, South Wales, a musical prodigy and a founder of seminal rock band, The Velvet Underground, is back in Britain for a short tour, giving the *Western Mail* an exclusive face-to-face interview.

Cale, the quiet young Welshman who went to America on a classical music scholarship and became a big noise in the '60s music scene, rubbing shoulders and nerve endings with Lou Reed and the late Andy Warhol, is looking good for his 50 years.

Tall, dark and dressed from head to toe in black, Cale is an intense man who savours carefully every question and nuance of conversation as we chat in his temporary 'home' in London's elegant Portobello Hotel.

After leaving Amman Valley Grammar School, Cale studied musicology at Goldsmith's College before a Leonard Bernstein scholarship took him to America.

There he performed with such influential avant-garde composers as John Cage and La Monte Young before teaming up with Lou Reed to form The Velvet Underground.

Now a resident of New York's Greenwich Village, Cale remains a creative genius. With Reed he helped create a new sound that unsettled the rock establishment of the '60s, before he quit to develop a solo career that has taken him on a world-wide tour of different musical genres.

He has been — and remains — a dark, introspective and enigmatic balladeer, a rock'n'roll firebrand, and a composer of everything from film scores to full-length ballets. Music remains his driving force . . .

Cale has been dubbed the 'godfather of punk' because of the

role The Velvet Underground played in the development of popular music.

He relaxes as he recalls the excitement of arriving in America after a boyhood in South Wales . . . A Welsh speaker, Cale is proud of his Welsh connections, visiting when he gets the chance his relatives in Pembrokeshire.

(John Cale talking to David Vickerman, *Western Mail*, 20 November 1992.)

By the mid-1980s a new era was opening for film makers in Wales, one in which television companies worked together with independent producers and directors. The English-language films of Karl Francis were the most widely distributed but the period was dominated by Welsh-language directors such as Endaf Emlyn whose *Hedd Wynn* was nominated for a Hollywood Academy Award in 1994. Ironically it was an American director, who later went on to make the very successful *Coming up Roses*, who first proved that the world was ready for Welsh-language cinema:

D.9   WELSH VOICES: AN AMERICAN IN THE VALLEYS

The director Stephen Bayly pays the rent on his sleek Covent Garden office with television commercials: he aims to do six a year (Vick's, the decongestant people, were recent clients). His heart, however, or at least a large part of it, is in the financially more constrained world of Welsh film-making, and he is modestly proud that his *Aderyn Papur* (. . . *And Pigs Might Fly*), which was shown at last year's London Film Festival, having picked up a raft of international awards, was the first subtitled Welsh-language feature shown on English television (Channel 4, 28 February). The BBC, he hopes, will shortly bestir itself and put out a subtitled version of his wartime drama series for S4C, *Joni Jones*. Bayly, an American long resident in Britain, and the Welsh producer Linda James founded the London-based production and distribution company Red Rooster Films two years ago. Their first feature, *Aderyn Papur* (literally 'Paper Bird'), found two mysterious Japanese arriving in a North Walian village and raising the hopes of a boy, whose dad is jobless and whose mother, as a result, has decamped to Liverpool, that work might, magically, be about to materialize. The Japanese, incidentally, who have no English, are utterly flummoxed by the Welsh and their language.

The company's second Welsh movie, *The Works*, which is now editing, again deals with work and the spectre of unemployment. It stars Dafydd Hywel, Brinley Jenkins and Iola Gregory (who has appeared in all three of Bayly's Welsh ventures); and, in the lead, Glenn Sherwood as a credulous youth embarking on his first job. Scripted in English by Kerry Crabbe and translated by Wilbert Lloyd Roberts (a veteran of the Welsh theatre), the story centres on a widget factory where computerisation threatens. It was shot double version chiefly in a gutted factory building in Aberdare, South Wales, at the end of last year.

The art director Hildegard Bechtler smartly transformed corners of the cavernous premises, but the overwhelming impression of the location, on a London visitor, was of chill desolation: an odd place to set a comedy.

'The real factory, Heliwell's, closed eight years ago,' Bayly said. 'It made exhaust pipes and was apparently doing well. But the owners decided to rationalize. The work was moved to another factory closer to the company's English headquarters and the machinery was sold to South Africa. No new employer has come to Aberdare since then. There were disconcerting echoes of this in our own story. When we arrived, and word got about, queues of applicants formed for jobs we couldn't provide . . .'

Stephen Bayly takes a strong campaigning interest in Welsh film-making. He has been learning Welsh for several years (languages come fairly easily and, seated in front of a Steenbeck, he fluently translates some Welsh dialogue from *The Works*); and he has made representation to his alma mater, the National Film and Television School, about the training of Welsh technicians. He himself took *The Works* to S4C; and Linda James extracted a 'top whack' budget of £220,000 from the Welsh channel ('Film on Four', if interested, might have paid more than £$\frac{1}{2}$ m) and then persuaded Channel 4, which had not previously co-financed a drama feature with its sister

S4C, to top this up with £100,000 for the English-language version.

There are, Bayly said, unaccustomed pitfalls awaiting the film-maker in Wales. 'One problem we had, shooting *The Works* double version, was welding a uniform English accent. Another was actually finding Welsh actors. There aren't many, and they're always in work. There are 43 speaking parts in *The Works* and I believe we employed every South Walian actor over the age of 40. One of the best jobs in the world is to be a Welsh actor.'

(John Pym, *Sight and Sound*, Vol. 54, No. 2, Spring 1985.)

Images of Wales

ROB HUMPHREYS

In 1988, the Welsh Affairs Committee of the House of Commons regretted the fact that Wales presented a series of distinct, and at times contrasting, images to the outside world and argued that prospects for increased economic investment would be helped if 'one face' of Wales could be presented and promoted. Whilst the suggestion that a unified image would help Welsh economic prospects is a fairly recent one, the observation that Wales has a multiplicity of images and that such a state of affairs is undesirable is neither original nor new. In 1921, Sir Alfred Zimmern astutely observed that there 'is not one Wales; there are three', those of 'Welsh Wales', 'English Wales' and 'American Wales' (*My Impressions of Wales*, London, 1921) and, in a major feature in the *Western Mail* in 1965, it was argued that Wales had 'three faces', though predictably enough they were different from those identified by Zimmern. Others have argued for a simpler, but powerful, 'two Wales' model of an 'inner' and 'outer' Wales (E.1), and Wales has popularly been seen as consisting of a series of dichotomies — be they north/ south, upland/lowland, rural/urban, or English-speaking/ Welsh-speaking.

E.1

The construction of a history of 'images', even for a relatively short period such as that since 1945, presents particular problems for the historian. Any history, including this one, whilst being about the past, also constitutes an image of that past in the present. A history of images of Wales also presents the historian with a mass of potential sources: images of Wales are created and re-created in Welsh political life, in art and literature

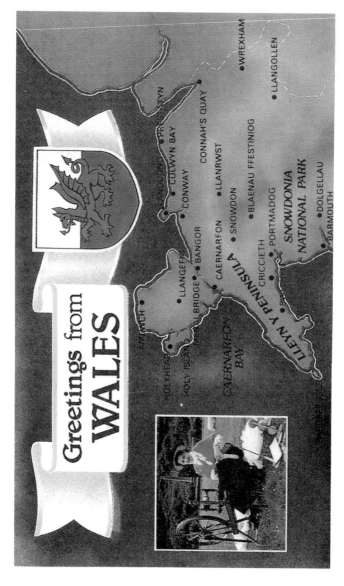

'Greetings from Wales'. (*Source: J. Arthur Dixon.*)

(whether written in Wales or outside Wales), on radio and in film and television productions, and — of ever increasing significance since 1945 — by and for tourists.

The picture is further complicated if we consider that all images of Wales carry their own in-built sense of the past — and sometimes of the future. Differing images of Wales in the present — whichever present that is — each have their own history which explains how that present has come about. Images of Wales in the future are sometimes constructed in order to illuminate the present, or in an attempt to provide political inspiration of some kind.

The exploration of the history of competing images of Wales can sometimes, therefore, seem like entering a hall of mirrors, particularly as historians inevitably, and unavoidably, reproduce an image of Wales in both the past and the present in their work. Indeed, it has been a feature of Welsh political and cultural life in the very recent past that historians have often intervened directly and explicitly in contemporary debates about the nature of Welsh images and identity and the processes by which they are produced. The issues of history and of time are therefore crucial and complex elements of any image of Wales. They rarely exist as unilinear processes, so therefore a history of images is one which is difficult to chronicle as a narrative sequence of events.

Nowhere is this better illustrated than in the success and longevity of the image of Wales presented in Richard Llewellyn's romantic novel *How Green Was My Valley*. Criticized in recent years for its nostalgic imagery and its subtle, and sometimes not so subtle, nationalist and anti-trade-union themes, it nevertheless remains, even in the 1990s, one of the dominant fictional representations of Wales, and of south Wales in particular. Yet the novel was published as long ago as 1939, and tells the story — via flashback — of the destruction of a mining family and community at the turn of the century (the exact chronological setting is never specified). Whatever the merits and shortcomings of Llewellyn's novel, the statement contained within it that the past can be 'as near as now' is certainly true of its own continued success — the novel has been both filmed and adapted for television, and has been reprinted many times in many languages — and of the image of Wales which it contains.

The broadcast, and subsequent publication in 1954, of Dylan Thomas's 'play for voices' *Under Milk Wood* marked the arrival of another dominant representation of Wales. Set in the fictional village of Llareggub, which Thomas described as a 'small town in a never never Wales', and a 'Wales which never was', the play's huge success has meant that it has taken on a life of its own, with many broadcasts, recordings and a stage version. Even Thomas himself, or at least the notion of him as a hard-drinking voluble Welshman (like Richard Burton who starred in the first broadcasting of the play), became the personification of one image of Wales. A valedictory article on Thomas which appeared shortly after his death reads like a parody of his own work but also locates the poet firmly in an already existing image of Wales as a land populated by myths, word-play and sing-song voices (E.2).

E.2

As with *How Green Was My Valley*, the poet and his work have enjoyed another 'career' after his death. As well as the production of a mass of critical material on both author and output, there is now a virtual Dylan Thomas industry of summer schools and conferences, in which 'Dylan Thomas Country' is marketed as a part of the tourist industry in south-west Wales. In the redeveloped Marina area of Swansea, a statue of the poet appears near a statue of one of his fictional characters (*Under Milk Wood*'s Captain Cat). History, fiction and image are fused together as a part of the economic reality of Wales of the 1990s.

The Wales of *Under Milk Wood* achieved greater purchase outside Wales, perhaps, where it had something in common with pre-existing romantic imagery which, in the wider sphere of British life, constituted an especially strong and long-lasting representation of Wales. This is an image which can be traced back to the writers and artists who visited the country in the late eighteenth and early nineteenth centuries, and who created in their work a Wales of sparsely populated hills and mountains, which inspired feelings of both inspiration and melancholy. Wales, to these writers and artists, was the repository of a way of life which had disappeared elsewhere (it shared this role with the Highlands of Scotland); it was a Wales which existed in contrast to, and in spite of, modernity itself. Some of the key 'views' of the Welsh landscape, which we now take for granted, were first 'framed' by painters of this period. Such views are constantly reproduced, as for example the depiction of the Aberglaslyn Pass in Snowdonia, painted by, amongst others, Francis Towne in 1777. This reappears in the photographer W.A. Poucher's 1949 volume *Wanderings in Wales*, and again in 1990 in the Wales Tourist Board's glossy *Journey Through Wales*, as well as on numerous picture postcards.

A similar kind of image of Wales has been reproduced in the work of artists and travel writers in the post-1945 period. Artists like John Piper and Graham Sutherland, leading members of what became known as a neo-Romantic movement, were attracted to the landscape of Wales because of its remoteness. For Sutherland, the preferred location was E.3 Pembrokeshire; for Piper it was Snowdonia (E.3, E.4). A E.4 native-born artist like Kyffin Williams also found inspiration in E.5 a 'melancholy' derived from the Welsh landscape (E.5). There is a not dissimilar theme running through the (little-explored) literature of mountaineering in Wales. The climber and political radical, Jim Perrin, has explained the attractions of the Welsh landscape, although actually talking about Snowdonia, in terms E.6 of romance and melancholy (E.6).

Although the dominant artistic representations of Wales continued to be those of rural — usually mountainous — landscapes, there were those who sought to depict other aspects of Welsh life. One such was Josef Herman, the Polish refugee who settled in the Swansea Valley mining village of Ystradgynlais in 1944. For Herman too, it was a vision of solitude which was initially the inspiration. More recent painters like George Chapman and Ernest Zobole, who do set out to depict the populated and the vibrant social experience of the Rhondda Valleys, are known, tellingly, as artists who create images of the Rhondda, as much as they are known as creators of images of Wales.

If the persistence of a romantic image of Wales was a central theme of the post-war period, one which perpetuated a vision of Wales as a territory — and sometimes a society — which had escaped the main features of modern life, it was matched by a countervailing image of a 'new Wales'. From 1945 until the mid-1960s the relative success of the reconstruction of the Welsh economy, informed and saturated as it was by the memory of the economic slump of the inter-war years, meant that renewal became a major theme of politics and policy-making (so much so that 'New South Wales' became for a while a Welsh as well as an Australian concept). Welsh politics, by now dominated by the Labour Party as a party of government, ran to wider British rhythms, so any attempt to extract images of such a Wales requires caution, and the temptation to use latter-day issues as organizing concepts has to be resisted. James Griffiths, who was later to become the first secretary of state for Wales and later still a supporter of an elected assembly for Wales, had said in 1945 that the most important question for the Welsh people in the preceding thirty years had been that

E.7 of 'livelihood' rather than self-government (E.7). A 'new' Wales, both in terms of aspiration and, to some extent at least, of achievement, was to be the main solution to this question.

The period was marked by a series of large-scale government-funded construction projects, such as the massive steel plants at Port Talbot and Llanwern (and the new housing developments that accompanied them); the M4 motorway; the building of (or plans for) new towns at Cwmbrân and, later, at Llantrisant and Newtown; and in the mid-1960s, the Severn Crossing. Each of these can now be identified as key images of the Wales of that period and, crucially, each was seen at the time of their construction as being symbolic of a 'new' Wales

E.8 and of the promise of a new prosperity (E.8). It was the steel industry above all, perhaps, which symbolized the reconstruction of south Wales. The Abbey plant at Port Talbot, with its high wages and the prospect of a job for life, became known locally as 'Treasure Island'. Writing in the early 1960s, the novelist and by then TV commentator, Gwyn Thomas, could even foresee a future in which the steel industry might enable the south Wales coastal strip to become another 'California'

E.9 (E.9). Even allowing for Thomas's well-developed sense of irony, this was a stunning mental re-creation of Zimmern's notion of 'American Wales'.

The optimism of the early 1950s, the continued social memory

The Abbey Works at Margam, Port Talbot, 1961. (*Source: Welsh Industrial and Maritime Museum.*)

of the 1930s and the extent to which the socialism of the Labour Party had moved into the mainstream were well captured in Paul Dickson's film *David*, made for the Festival of Britain in 1951. The Festival was intended to demonstrate to the world and to the people of Britain the cultural, artistic and technological achievements and continued potential of the British. To some extent, therefore, Dickson's film might be seen as an 'official' image of Wales at that time. The film tells the story of an ex-miner, now school caretaker (played by, and based on the life of, the brother of James Griffiths), who loses his son but whose contribution in a pastoral sense to the boys at his school as they

E.10   progress to a better future gives meaning to his life (E.10). The similarities and contrasts with *How Green was My Valley* are striking. As in Llewellyn's novel, the film uses flashback to tell us of the suffering of a family but this is a story of loss which leads, via commitment and solidarity, to a better world, one which at the same time does not sever its links with the past.

As the economic settlement of the post-war era began to unravel in the 1970s and as it was at least partially dismantled under the Tory governments in the 1980s, what was once a new and future Wales became something which, for some, had to be defended. In the 1980s and early 1990s, there were again voices raised in support of a 'new Wales' but this time the voices came from the right.

This new 'new Wales' is, like the 'new Wales' of the 1950s, as much aspiration as it is achievement. It is informed by a rejection of some of the successes of the post-war reconstruction, coupled with an environmental concern which is able to celebrate the decline of the coal industry because it has led to a re-greening of south Wales, and a removal of a 'psychological incubus that affected the quality of life' in that part of Wales (David Cole (ed.), *The New Wales*, Cardiff, 1990, p.5.)

Not everyone in the 1950s and 1960s viewed the prospect of the new post-war Wales (still less a 'Californian' Wales) with optimism. For a growing number of nationalist writers and intellectuals, the nature and pace of change, and the affluence which was created as a consequence of that change, did not represent a better future. This was not progress, it was argued, but instead it entailed the destruction of a set of values and way of life which were distinctly Welsh, to be replaced by an Anglo-American materialism. These writers and intellectuals imagined a Wales in which the Welsh language was the key — often the only — marker of Welshness. The language was already under threat or in decline but it also held the promise of an escape from mass culture and rootlessness. There are echoes here of the romantic Wales of the tourist industry, but it is the culture, or at least one part of it, rather than the landscape which is central and, in any case, tourism itself is often identified as a threat to that culture.

As this kind of debate about the nature of Wales and Welshness gathered pace during the 1960s, a process aided by an initial slowing down of the economic gains which had been made in the 1950s, and later by the onset of real economic problems, a key influence was Saunders Lewis. In his 1967 play *Cymru Fydd* (Tomorrow's Wales) he used the notion of a future Wales in order to warn against the loss of the dual and interwoven phenomena of spiritual and moral values and Welsh identity, in the face of an encroaching American mass culture. Lewis's 1962 rallying-call lecture *Tynged Yr Iaith* (The Fate of the Language) had already made it plain that it was the language above all else which had to be rescued if Wales was to survive. The resultant formation of Cymdeithas yr Iaith Gymraeg (the Welsh Language Society) led to a sustained campaign of direct action in support of the Welsh language, but it also created a striking and lasting visual image of Wales in the 1960s, that of English-only place-names and road signs being daubed with paint and replaced with Welsh versions. That image itself contains three sub-images: a Welsh-language Wales; an English-language Wales; and the matter of Wales and Welshness being a source of conflict.

The coupling of the Welsh language and Welsh identity was a central component of this imagined Wales. A decline in the language was therefore by definition a decline in Welshness itself. The Swansea-based philosopher J. R. Jones (another important influence on Cymdeithas yr Iaith Gymraeg) painted a moving and poignant mental image of Wales and the culture which it represents, evaporating in the face of the encroachment of the English (E.11). This image spoke of a real crisis of

E.11

economy, particularly of housing, in rural Wales, as well as of cultural developments.

The vision of a rootless mass replacing the organic social pattern of the 'real' Wales was also a recurring theme — at least for intellectuals and language activists — in the 1960s and 1970s. This fate for Wales could be avoided, it was claimed by some, by the growth of the Welsh language which could act as a bulwark

E.12 against destructive Anglo-American influences (E.12). Of course, during that period and since, many young Welsh speakers have sought to create a modern popular, and pop, culture in the Welsh language, rather than rejecting that kind of world.

Perhaps the most striking feature of this idealized Welsh-language Wales which was being produced and propagated in the 1960s was that a new generation of writers who wrote in the English language also subscribed to this view. For these writers, the Welsh language and the value system which — as they saw it — went with it, had the potential to lead the majority (English monoglot) part of the Welsh population away from impoverished mass culture to a more enlightened (and Welsh) life and culture. This, too, involved an image of an idealized Wales which these writers had been attracted to in the first instance and which was in turn reproduced in their work.

A key influence here was the poet R.S. Thomas, who from the late 1940s had produced a sustained series of poems which portrayed Wales as an essentially rural culture now under threat and showing symptoms of serious — at times seemingly irre-trievable — decay, as a result of alien, usually English, influences. Born in Cardiff and having learned Welsh as an adult, Thomas had journeyed both in reality and in his imagination as he went in

E.13 search of a 'real' Wales (E.13). From the late 1960s, Thomas moved on to other issues as subject matter for his verse, but his work on the matter of Wales became some of the best-known poems written since the war, often included in anthologies and used as set texts in schools long after they were first written.

The image of a Wales in which the Welsh language was the defining characteristic of Welshness inevitably led to an image of Wales — for some a political aim — in which the English language, and those who spoke it, occupied a highly ambiguous

E.14
E.15

position. At times, they could be portrayed with patronizing contempt (E.14); at others, as having a secondary role in a possible future flowering of Welsh identity (E.15).

This image of an idealized Welsh-language Wales was very prominent in Welsh cultural and artistic life in the 1960s and 1970s, although it is harder to judge how far it had any purchase on the vast majority of the Welsh people, whatever language they spoke. It would appear reasonable to suggest that an image of Wales which sought, to a greater or lesser extent, to denigrate the achievements of the 'new Wales' of the post-war years was never going to attract support outside a relatively small, if vocal, group of intellectuals. Certainly, the debate around Welshness which had gathered pace since the 1960s played some, but by no means the only, part in the abrupt rejection of the proposals for devolution of power to Wales in 1979.

The period since 1979 has seen existing images of Wales produced and reproduced, and new ones created. As the Welsh Affairs Committee discovered, the image of 'short dark men singing hymns in the shadow of slag heaps', which owes as much to film and fiction as it does to historical fact, can still be a powerful and partial representation of the Welsh, even when slag-heaps and coal-miners have all but disappeared. But it can also coexist with an image of Wales as a land 'dripping with microchips' — again more image than actuality — which would have been inconceivable just a few years ago (Welsh Affairs Committee, *Inward Investment into Wales and its Interaction with Regional and EEC Policies*, Vol. 1, 1988, para.39).

One image which came to the fore in the 1980s was that of a land in which image itself was a matter of debate and argument. The question mark became grafted on to the word 'Wales' and 'Welsh' with some frequency. Historians published books with the titles *Wales! Wales?* and *When Was Wales?*, and a sociologist enquired 'What is Wales?' The growth in Welsh historical writing since the 1960s, particularly that which dealt with the previously underexplored history of industrial Wales, meant that historians were well placed to contribute to this debate, and to uncover the processes by which images of Wales are produced. In the act of writing history, of course, historians also reproduce their own images of both the Welsh past and the Welsh present. That different interpretations were possible was strikingly revealed in the early 1980s, when two of the most prominent historians of modern Wales used images of rebirth, as in Kenneth O. Morgan's *Rebirth of a Nation: Wales 1880–1980*, and of death, as in Gwyn A. Williams's *When Was Wales?*, to describe Wales in the late twentieth century.

The idea that prevailing images of Wales and the Welsh now need to be jettisoned or renewed, either because they fail to reflect things as they actually are, or because they serve the interests of others, has also been a frequent subject of debate in the 1980s. Popular stereotypes have been challenged, and the Welsh themselves criticized, as in Nigel Jenkins's poem 'Land
E.16   of Song' (E.16), and Wales itself has been imagined as 'comically scattered' but also as feminine in Menna Elfyn's 'Siapiau o
E.17   Gymru' (E.17). If Richard Burton, Cliff Morgan and Dylan Thomas once themselves constituted images of Wales within popular culture, we can now point to a somewhat more eclectic series of national icons of this kind, be they Sir Anthony Hopkins, Shirley Bassey or Colin Jackson. The conversion of some Nonconformist chapels — at one time of course an important marker of Welshness — into business premises in recent years is highly symbolic of the fact that Wales is now a secular society. The conversion of two such chapels in Cardiff into mosques is symbolic of the fact that Wales is a multicultural society and more than bilingual.

Yet a romantic image of Wales persists. The rapid decline and near disappearance of the Welsh coalfield has enabled that industry to be incorporated, to some extent, into the ever-expanding tourist industry. It is now possible to visit a range of 'heritage attractions' which seek to portray the history of coal-mining and other industries in Wales, and images of the coalfield, whether winding gear, miners themselves, or even trade-union banners, are now, for the first time, produced and purchased as cultural artefacts. This development has led to the issues of historical accuracy, the form of modern museums, and the prospects for employment growth from tourism often being unhelpfully interwoven. Images and icons of coal and slate are ubiquitous — even though very few Welsh people are now employed in those industries — as are many other items of

Wales, the 'Land of a Thousand Castles'. (*Source: J. Arthur Dixon.*)

tourist ephemera, such as dragons and love-spoons. Yet in another, important, sense, these are not ephemeral. Whatever the arguments about the quality of employment opportunities in tourism, the fact remains that images of Wales are now an important — and real — sector of the economy.

Despite the fact that the tendency of the tourist industry is to seek to unify 'Wales' into a single image, there can be no doubt that the Welsh will continue to create images of themselves in a multitude of ways, and that the media by and through which these images are produced will also change, as developments in electronic communications and information technology gather pace. There is also no doubt that images will continue to be produced of Wales and the Welsh by others. Questions about the accuracy of those images, of who produces them, and for what purpose, will, inevitably, continue to be posed.

Sources

E.1   In the end it is the culture of Inner Wales that has given Wales its personality, its language, its religion and song. These survive into the modern epoch and represent the real Wales . . . the continuation of Welsh life and culture in the inner zone depends to a very large extent on the ability of the mountains to defend the culture of valleys facing the west and north. We are, however, living in an age that can override geographical obstacles with ease. What was begun by the railways and carried forward by the trunk roads and the motor car, is completed with the coming of radio and television. Geographical factors are losing their potency, for at the present time mountains, as such, provide neither shelter nor protection. These obstructions have been surmounted. Our cosmopolitan civilization can now reach into the farthest west. Is there a danger that the old inner stronghold of Welsh life and culture can be overrun by modern cosmopolitan culture? This is the problem that faces Wales today.

(E.G. Bowen, *The Geography of Wales as a Background to its History*, originally broadcast in Welsh as the Annual Radio Lecture on

BBC Radio Wales, 14 May 1964. This excerpt taken from I. Hume and W.T.R. Pryce, *The Welsh and their Country*, Llandysul, Gomer, 1986, pp.85–7.)

E.2 But the first thing about Dylan was that he was Welsh. Like all Celts he had that lovely gift of the gab which could set a company of field-mice hiccuping like haycocks with extravagance. Words sang for him, and that is the birthmark of a poet. Dylan preferred sound sense to sound sense, if you know what I mean . . .

For Dylan was not just a warm wild sly quick red fox of a Celt; he was also, by birth, a Calvinist, reared among the doom-telling, bell-tolling hymn-roofed Presbyterian chapels of Wales . . .

He never lost his affection for Wales, for the wildly unruly ways of its warm-blooded men and women with their earth-bound practices (just listen to the broadcast of 'Under Milk Wood'), nor did he ever have less than liking for their strict impossible rules and their heavenbound faith . . .

(W.R. Rogers, 'Dylan Thomas', *Spectator*, 27 May 1954, p.913.)

E.3 These valleys possess a bud-like intricacy of form and contain streams, often of indescribable beauty, which run to the sea. The astonishing fertility of these valleys and the complexity of the roads running through them is a delight to the eye. The roads form strong and mysterious arabesques as they rise in terraces, in sight, hidden, turning and splitting as they finally disappear into the sky. To see a solitary human figure descending such a road at the solemn moment of sunset is to realize the enveloping quality of the earth, which can create, as it does here, a mysterious space limit — a womb-like enclosure — which gives the human form an extraordinary focus and significance . . .

(Graham Sutherland, letter to Sir Colin Anderson, published in *Horizon*, 1942. Quoted in Malcolm Yorke, *The Spirit of Place*, London, Constable, 1988, p.116.)

E.4   Mist blowing across all day: visibility about 15–20 yards only; curious sensation in presence of gigantic boulders, giant coffin slabs, pale trunk-shaped rocks, disappearing into grey invisibility even at close range. The affectionate nature of the mountain is not changed by the acute loneliness and closed-in feeling induced by the mist: but an atmosphere of an affectionate cemetery.

(John Piper, 'Note written near the summit of Glyder Fawr', *c.*1950, appears in Tate Gallery catalogue *John Piper*, 1983, Tate Gallery Publications; quoted in I. B. Rees (ed.), *The Mountains of Wales*, Cardiff, University of Wales Press, 1992, p.212.)

E.5   My Welsh inheritance must always remain a strong force in my work, for it is Wales that I can paint with the greatest freedom. I have worked in Holland, France and Austria, in Italy and in Greece, but in none of these lovely countries have I found the mood that touches the seam of melancholy that is within most Welshmen, a melancholy that derives from the dark hills, the heavy clouds and the enveloping sea mists.

(Kyffin Williams, *Across the Straits*, London, Duckworth, 1973, p.159.)

E.6   The landscape of Wales has a powerful appeal to incurable romantics (or natural depressives?) such as myself. Perhaps it is the attraction of the marginal — the rough hills and crags, the ravaged industries, the legend-teeming sunset seas on which imagination sets the mortally wounded king's barge floating out to Avalon. And a culture which still rages, to keep its light from dying.

(Jim Perrin, 'The Gilded Calamity', in *On and Off the Rocks*, London, Victor Gollancz, 1986, p.13.)

E.7   The major problem that has preoccupied our people during the last thirty years is that of securing a livelihood. Welsh community life was being increasingly undermined by the economic disintegration that was the consequence of the breakdown of

Above Carneddi 2 by Kyffin Williams. (Source: Kyffin Williams/National Library of Wales.)

Monopoly Capitalism. For almost the whole of the inter-war period mass unemployment and its consequent insecurity and poverty was the curse that paralysed Welsh life. The Government has worked hard and with a degree of success towards the reconstruction of our economy . . . I repeat to you what I said in the House that a separate Government would be a disaster for our people.

(James Griffiths, letter to Mr Trevor Roberts of Grove Cottage Garnant, 1948?, James Griffiths Papers C2/25, National Library of Wales.)

E.8   TOWN BECOMES CENTRE OF STEEL WORLD

Dream realized with opening of Abbey Works
Most important day in Port Talbot's history

. . . the people of the world . . . have for a long time watched with interest the growth of the steel Colossus, the old borough which had given it birth bathed in the glory of recognized achievement . . .

It was a day touching in its symbolism. When Mr Gaitskill pushed over a lever in the rolling mill and sent a slab of red-hot steel on its way towards providing another motor car, refrigerator, tank or perambulator . . .

(*Port Talbot Guardian*, 20 July 1951.)

E.9   In a community based on great industries that can be twisted out of shape in a generation, change is bound to be convulsive and erratic. Much of South Wales does less than justice to her people. Socially far too much of its life is sub-standard. But its economic prospects are so bright as to make imperative vast and rapid strides in dealing with the stupid horse-collar of nine-teenth-century squalor and inadequacy that still hangs about our neck. Within the framework of such steel centres as Llanwern, Port Talbot and Ebbw Vale, the place could become a buzzing and brilliant California.

(Gwyn Thomas, *A Welsh Eye*, London, Hutchinson, 1964, 1984 edition, p.158.)

E.10 My name is Ifor Morgan . . . and I've come home. There at my feet is the town where I was born. What do I remember best in this little town? . . . if you asked me anyone in particular I'd say old Dafydd Rhys, the caretaker at the County School. There was a Welshman indeed to remember. If I tell you about him you'll remember I think . . .

DAFYDD You see, Ifor, it was different for us in those days. We had no choice. Most men of my age in Wales can tell the same story. Getting coal was our wealth and our destiny . . . I wanted to grow up to be like these men. I wanted to be strong as they were. To be able to laugh deep in my throat the way they did. And I wanted to hate the fireman the way they did.

FIREMAN Come on you men. Let's have another strong prop here.

GAFFER Get away man. What d'you think we're building — the new Jerusalem?

DAFYDD It was a hard life, but I knew no other . . .

DAFYDD When I came off my last shift, my son was there to meet me. He was grown up now and was getting a good education. There were new opportunities for the young men in Wales, and I wanted him to succeed where I had failed.

(*David/Dafydd*, written and directed by Paul Dickson for World Wide Pictures Ltd, 1951. Unpublished script in British Film Institute library, London.)

E.11 Dywedir am un profiad ei fod yn un o'r rhai mwyaf ingol sy'n bod . . . sef gorfod gadael daear eich gwlad am byth, troi cefn ar eich treftadaeth, cael eich rhwygo allan gerfydd y gwraidd o dir eich cynefin. 'Chefais i mo'r profiad hwn y diau nas cawsoch chwithau. Ond mi wn i am brofiad arall sydd yr un mor ingol, ac yn fwy anesgor (oblegid mi fedrech ddychwelyd i'ch cynefin), a hwnnw yw'r profiad o wybod, nid eich bod chwi yn gadael eich gwlad, ond fod eich gwlad yn eich gadael chwi, yn darfod allan o fod o dan eich traed chwi, yn cael ei sugno i ffwrdd oddiwrthych, megis gan lyncwynt gwancus, i ddwylo ac i feddiant gwlad a gwareiddiad arall.

(J.R. Jones, *Gwaedd yng Nghymru*, Lerpwl, Cyhoeddiadau Modern Cymreig, 1970; quoted in J. Osmond (ed.), *The National Question Again: Welsh Political Identity in the 1980s*, Llandysul, Gomer, 1985, p.184.)

(It is said of one experience that it is one of the most agonising possible . . . that of having to leave the soil of your own country forever, of turning your back on your heritage, being torn away from the roots of your familiar land. I have not suffered that experience. But I know of an experience equally agonising and more irreversible (for you could return to your home), and that is the experience of knowing, not that you are leaving your country, but that your country is leaving you, is ceasing to exist under your very feet, being sucked away from you, as it were by a consuming, swallowing wind, into the hands and the possession of another country and civilisation.)

(Trans. in Phylip Rosser, 'Growing Through Political Change', ibid., p.185.)

E.12   But our standpoint is this: there would be no reality to a self-governing Wales, even one which possessed every possible political institution, if it did not also have the Welsh language. Further, it would not have an atom of strength to withstand the Anglo-American influences flooding into it through commercial advertising and in the mass media, nor to resist the worst excesses of the predatory capitalism with which the near future threatens us. In a word, the destruction of the Welsh national identity would be inevitable, despite its political institutions; nothing would be left but a superficial and shortlived regional awareness . . .

If the Welsh language were to die, and so share the fate that is likely to overtake some other numerically small cultures

before the end of this century, humanity would be impoverished in the sense that one thread among the thousands that
make up the cultural pattern of mankind — whose glory is its
variety — would be lost. We see this linguistic and cultural
diversity also as a defence against the shallowness and corrup-
tion of the Anglo-American anti-culture that pours into every
corner of the world through the machinery of capitalism. It is in
this cultural and national diversity that we see a means of satis-
fying man's need for roots.

(Cymdeithas yr Iaith Gymraeg, Maniffesto, trans. Harri Webb,
1972, *Planet*, No. 26/27, Winter 1974/75, pp.84–5.)

E.13   There was a vacant parish in English Maelor at the time, and
since it provided a suitable house, there we went, into what
might as well have been the English plain — that part of
Flintshire which lies between Wrexham and Cheshire. And
from there, in the evening I could see the Welsh hills some
fifteen miles away in the evening, magical and mysterious as
ever. I realized what I had done. My place was not here on this
plain amongst these Welsh with English accents and attitudes. I
set about learning Welsh, so as to get back to the real Wales of
my imagination.

(R.S. Thomas, *Y Llwybrau Gynt 2* (The Paths Gone By), 1972, in
S. Anstey (ed.), *R.S. Thomas: Selected Prose*, Poetry Wales Press,
1986.)

E.14   Yrg nghegin gefn ei dŷ mae'n cadw cenedl,
Lletywr rhad na chyst ond lle i'w wely
Ac yn y parlwr ef ei hun sy'n byw, yn Sais ail-law
A'i ffenestri'n lled agored tua'r byd. Ba waeth
Os yw ei ben yn bwn, a chur y tu ôl
I'w glustiau? Y mae'r gwynt yn iach ysgubol,
Ac nid oes lysiau ar ôl i'w diwreiddio mwy
O'i ardd, dim ond cancr y llwybrau concrit.

Gwyn fyd yr alltud 'gaiff ymestyn mewn parlwr
A llygadu'r bydysawd maith o lwybrau llaethog —

Llwybrau llaeth a mêl.
Gallai, fe allai aros byth a syllu arnynt,
A llyfu diwylliant lleng heb feddu'r un,
Llwybrau llyfn. Pam mae ei wddf
Wedi ei nyddu ar un ochr i'w gwylied hwy
Fel pwped yn hongian ar hoel ar ôl y gyngerdd,
A'i geg ar lled, a lleufer yn y llygaid? Paham?

(Bobi Jones, 'Cymro Di-Gymraeg', 1965, in Bobi Jones,
Casgliad o Gerddi, Abertawe, Cyhoeddiadau Barddas, 1989,
pp.100–1.)

(In the back kitchen of his house he keeps a nation,
A cheap lodger who costs no more than a place for his bed,
And he himself lives in the parlour, a second-hand Saxon,
His windows wide open to the world. What matter
If his head is a burden, and there is a throbbing
Behind his ears? The wind is brisk and sweeping,
And there are no plants left to be uprooted
From his garden, only the cancer of concrete paths.

Happy the exile who can stretch out in a parlour
And eye the vast universe of milky ways —
Ways of milk and honey.
Yes, he could stay gazing at them forever,
Licking a legion's culture without possessing it,
Smooth paths. Why is his neck
Twisted to one side to watch them
Like a puppet hanging on a nail after the performance,
Its mouth agape and a gleam in the eyes? Why?)

(Bobi Jones, 'A Welshless Welshman', in *Bobi Jones, Selected
Poems*, trans. Joseph P. Clancy, Swansea, Christopher Davies,
1987, p.90.)

E.15   ... but English-speaking Wales is in a different situation. It is a
province slowly coming back to life and looking for something
to replace the second-rate greyness of its life. If enough people
attach themselves to the notion of Wales, if enough talent stays

in the country and devotes itself to building a better society here, then changes will come. The people who make such a movement, whatever their first language, are bound to look for support to the Welsh language culture which conserves the Welsh tradition unbroken.

(Ned Thomas, *The Welsh Extremist*, London, Victor Gollancz, 1971; from Y Lolfa edition, 1973, pp.119–20.)

E.16   Oggy! Oggy! Oggy!
This is the music
of the Welsh machine
programmed — Oggy! — to sing
non-stop, and to think only
that it thinks it thinks
when it thinks in fact nothing.

Sing on, machine, sing
in your gents-only bar —
you need budge not an inch
to vanquish the foe,
to ravish again
the whore of your dreams,
to walk songful and proud
through the oggy oggy toyland
of Oggy Oggy Og.

Sing with the blinding hwyl
of it all: you are programmed
to sing: England expects —
my hen laid a haddock
and all that stuff.

Ar hyd y nos, ar hyd
y dydd — the songs, the songs,
the hymns and bloody arias
that churn from its mouth
like puked-up S.A. —

and not a word meant,
not a word understood
by the Welsh machine.

Oggy! Oggy! Oggy!
shame dressed as pride.
The thing's all mouth,
needs a generous boot
up its oggy oggy arse
before we're all of us sung
into oggy oggy silence.

(Nigel Jenkins, 'Land of Song (I.m. 1.iii.79)', 1979, in Meic
Stephens (ed.), *The Bright Field*, Manchester, Carcanet, 1991,
p.168.)

E.17   Ei diffinio rown
        ar fwrdd glân,
        rhoi ffurf i'w ffiniau,
        ei gyrru i'w gororau
        mewn inc coch;
        ac meddai myfyriwr o bant
        'It's like a pig running away';
        wedi bennu chwerthin,
        rwy'n ei chredu;
        y swch gogleddol
        yn heglu'n gynt
        na'r swrn deheuol
        ar ffo rhag y lladdwyr.

        Siapiau yw hi siŵr iawn:
        yr hen geg hanner rhwth
        neu'r fraich laes ddiog
        sy'n gorffwys ar ei rhwyfau;
        y jwmpwr, wrth gwrs,
                    ar ei hanner,
        gweill a darn o bellen ynddi,
        ynteu'n debyg i siswrn

parod i'w ddarnio'i hun;
cyllell ddeucarn anturiaethydd,
neu biser o bridd
craciedig a gwag.

A lluniau amlsillafog
yw'r tirbeth o droeon
a ffeiriaf â'm cydnabod
a chyda'r estron
sy'n ei gweld am yr hyn yw:
ddigri o wasgaredig
sy
am
fy
mywyd
      fel bwmerang diffael yn mynnu
           mynnu
        ffeindio'i
      ffordd
    yn
ôl
at
fy nhraed.

(Menna Elfyn, 'Siapiau o Gymru', 1986, in Menna Elfyn, *Aderyn Bach Mewn Llaw: Cerddi 1976–90*, Llandysul, Gwasg Gomer, 1990, pp.98–9.)

(I was defining her
on a clean slate
fleshing out her frontiers
badgering her to her borders
in red ink;
when a foreign student said:
"It's like a pig running away";
laughing done with,
I believe her;
the northern snout
hoofing it faster

than her southern rump,
fleeing her slaughterers.

she's made of shapes, you know:

the slack old mouth, agape
or the lazy, lolling arm,
resting on its oars;
the jumper, of course,
            half done,
wrapped around a bit of wool and the needles,
or else, she's a pair of scissors
ready to ribbon herself,
an adventurer's double-hafted knife,
or an earthen pitcher,
hollow and cracked.

she's polysyllabled pictures,
this inleted landmass
I swap with acquaintances
and with the foreigner
who sees her for what she is:
comically scattered,
who is
on my life
like an unerring boomerang which wills
                    which wills
             its way
          always
       back
    to
  my
feet.)

(Menna Elfyn, 'The Shapes she Makes', trans. Elin ap Hywel, in
Ceri Meyrick (ed.), *The Bloodstream*, Bridgend, Seren Books,
1989, pp.52–3.)

Constructing the Severn Bridge, c.1965. (Source: *Welsh Industrial and Maritime Museum*.)

Wales and the Wider World

CHRISTOPHER HARVIE

Wales and the Human Condition

F.1

'An upheaval from being's very roots . . . gurgling up hot lava suddenly on to the green grass.' I begin with a quotation from a Welsh novelist — Welsh by self-election rather than origin — in a work which has a claim to be one of the great fictional treatments of European politics (F.1). Richard Hughes, in a trilogy *The Human Condition*, of which only two books, *The Fox in the Attic* (1961) and *The Wooden Shepherdess* (1973), were actually completed, tried to create a picture of European politics after the trauma of the First World War. In these works the problems of both a depressed industrial and an archaic rural Wales could be related to those socio-political breakdowns in continental Europe which had produced the Nazis.

At the core of the first volume he uses this vivid metaphor. Where does Wales fit into this? Perhaps that sense of personal identity at the core of the 'we–they' contrast might be contained and managed where the 'we' is small-scale, non-Utopian, bound by language, culture, and the accessible local community. And this may have been Hughes's intention when, after a life spent roving through post-Versailles Europe and recording the impact of the Second World War, he returned to Talgarth, near Harlech, where he undertook this last project.

In his ambitions for *The Human Condition*, Hughes seems to reflect the contrasts visible in Wales's twentieth-century international career. At one level the Welsh, the Welsh-born, or activists and organizations based in Wales, have played a disproportionate role in world politics: think of Lloyd George,

the saviour of Britain in the First World War and one of the
architects (for better or worse) of the ethnic-national Europe of
the Versailles settlement; or of the Fabian Thomas Jones, influencing the entourage of Baldwin and MacDonald in a liberal,
post-imperial direction. Aneurin Bevan's efforts to thaw the
Cold War in the 1950s were similarly concerned with international affairs, as was James Callaghan's use of his links with
Henry Kissinger in the mid-1970s.

More moralistic were Lord Davies's benefactions to the
League of Nations movement, in Wales and beyond: the inter-
national relations chair at the University College of Wales,
Aberystwyth, and the Temple of Peace and Health in Cathays
Park, were inaugurated in the otherwise ominous year of 1937.
In the 1960s and after, the country's peace tradition helped give
rise to the Campaign for Nuclear Disarmament, Bertrand
Russell and the Committee of 100 and, later on, to the
Greenham Common women. After the war, and increasing in
influence in the 1970s, there was the Austrian Leopold Kohr's
'small is beautiful' philosophy, affecting the Green and envi-
ronmentalist movement, and Plaid Cymru.

But in this process of influence, the springs of action are not
always straightforwardly political or rational. What the
American historian Daniel J. Boorstin publicized as the 'image'
also mattered. Visiting the Dolgellau Eisteddfod in 1949, Sir
Reginald Coupland was struck by how foreign it clearly was,
and in general by the interest of the Welsh in international as
F.2   well as in Welsh affairs (F.2). From the 1940s, in embryo, and
since the 1970s in actuality, Wales has become a field of inter-
change for European regionalist movements. This has cultural
origins, owing much to Plaid Cymru's interest in other
European culture-nations, its defence of Breton nationalists
from post-war revanchism, and to the international links of the
National Eisteddfod and Urdd Gobaith Cymru, elaborated
after 1947 by the Llangollen International Eisteddfod. More
recently it has taken on a cross-party focus, with the political
and economic concept of a 'Europe of the Regions', bound up
with the attraction of inward investment and the transfer of
F.3   high technology (F.3). Yet it still retains deep and complex
cultural roots.

How, for example, do we judge the effect on the international 'recognition' of Wales, of Dylan Thomas, in his recordings, broadcasts, and the tours that eventually killed him? A poem like 'Fern Hill' (F.4) both transposed the language of the chapel into a sort of rustic hedonism, and equated the small community with an age of innocence, something which had a huge appeal in the post-war anglophone world. Thomas was apolitical when sober, and had no time for Welsh nationalism — 'my opinion of Welsh nationalism can be expressed in three words, two of which are Welsh nationalism' — but his 'image' and his poems helped generate that vague but potent discontent with modern materialism and the military-industrial society that was summed up by the songs of one American disciple, Bob Zimmerman of Minnesota, who took the name Bob Dylan.

F.4

Dylan Thomas was of the first generation explicitly to regard themselves as Anglo-Welsh. Much of his early poetry was published in Keidrich Rhys's *Wales*, whose programme shows that his contemporaries were conscious of the Irish and Scottish renaissances, and already suspicious of the metropolis — although Rhys ran his journal from one pub or another in Soho (F.5). That sense of an independent voice — of being 'at a slight angle to the universe', as E.M. Forster described another 'hybrid' writer, the Alexandrian Greek C.F. Cafavy — provided resources for international communication denied to a monoglot Welsh culture, albeit at a price.

F.5

As Philip Cooke and his Cardiff colleagues show, the sort of regional-internationalism that this has enabled is now directly affecting the lives of many Welsh people (F.3). A sense of dialogue with other societies, in which the metropolis, with its coercive power and its arrogance, is sidelined, has rapidly developed over the last two decades. Lord Elis Thomas has written of an 'informal' Welsh constitution evolving, largely thanks to external recognition of the country's distinctiveness (F.6).

F.3

F.6

On the other hand it is less easy to locate the precise 'Welshness' of the political element of these movements. Wales has had an impressive record in stocking Westminster front-benches, in terms of seats and personalities: as leaders of the Labour party, Keir Hardie, Ramsay MacDonald, James Callaghan, Michael Foot and Neil Kinnock sat for Welsh constituencies. Aneurin Bevan, James Griffiths, Roy Jenkins and Merlyn Rees were no less important as Labour front-benchers. Until recently the Scottish performance was far more modest. Is this simply to do with the fact that it is physically possible to pursue a London political career and rapidly get back to a rock-solid south Wales seat when necessary — something which may or may not rub off on the actual electorate? What is specifically Welsh about Bevan's stint as Labour shadow foreign secretary, 1956–61? Given his ferocity in opposing ideas of Welsh self-government, how does he differ from a non-resident Welshman such as Sir Geoffrey Howe, Lord Howe of Aberavon, as foreign minister, 1983–8?

The Stateless Nation

F.6   At this point we must ask some basic questions. Wales is a nation which seems to be acquiring a state of sorts (F.6). How? What role has formal politics played in this? What economic motivations have lain behind it? What social and cultural institutions? And, finally, what critical political struggles have brought it about?

The state-nation issue is central. Because of the debate about how much of a nation, or how many nations, Wales is, or was, Gwyn A. Williams's famous meditation about Wales, nation-hood and time, in *When Was Wales?* ended on a deeply

F.7   pessimistic note (F.7). Written in 1985, this bears the scar of the twin defeats of the 1979 referendum and the miners' strike — perhaps also of the rise to Labour leadership of Neil Kinnock, a politician of markedly unionist views. But notice also the symbolism — always something to be looked for in the Celts: 'There's more enterprise | In walking naked' was how W.B. Yeats (borrowing from Carlyle's *Sartor Resartus?*) concluded the poem quoted by Gwyn A. Williams. This suggests a more posit-ive outcome: the need for a periodic reassessment of the national condition — throwing off old clothes.

We can apply the same sort of analysis to Denis Balsom, who slightly earlier, had produced his 'Three Wales Model' (in John Osmond (ed.), *The National Question Again*, Llandysul, 1983).

Less pessimistic, for it took into account the regional success of Plaid Cymru, this still suggested a limited future for Wales as a unit. Did time or social fractures portend the Welsh nation shrunk to a *1066 and All That* or *Sun*-reader level of rugby fifteens, women in funny hats, complicated place-names and over-simple surnames? (For Scotland see kilts, golf, whisky, meanness and the Loch Ness Monster.) Perhaps not: Balsom may have had J.B. Priestley's notion of 'four Englands' in mind, from his *English Journey* (1934): historic England, Victorian England, modern England and derelict England. This did not in itself deny any English capacity to cohere, but it shows (as with Gwyn A. Williams's naked people) a tendency to borrow English (or Irish or Scottish) cultural and literary models to try to define Welsh identity. By contrast, Northern Ireland is different again. Not only is it difficult to make jokes about terrorism, but no one (in Germany, say) is ever likely to call Dr Ian Paisley English — although they were perfectly capable of calling Neil Kinnock thus.

Arguably, this problem is transitory. States fit into a structure of international representation which defines them. They have embassies, delegations and diplomats; they are allocated space in the standard works of reference produced by the United Nations and other bodies. When these institutions are absent, cultural and political factors count for more, but these have a directional definition: they register with some receivers, but not with others. Hence the paradox that while the traditional markers of Welsh distinctiveness — the indigenous nature of the population, language, religion — have been either in decline or struggling to hold their own, the international distinctiveness of the nation has increased. The Council for Wales and Monmouthshire in 1948, followed by the Welsh Office in 1964, have incrementally created a political focus in Cardiff which was able to make good even the setback of the 1979 referendum. Many more would now follow Raymond Williams in describing themselves as Welsh European, than, say, twenty-five years ago.

Party Positions

Do the Welsh still identify with Britain? At one time this would have been unquestioned. Now it seems much more to do with party and culture. Dr John Redwood, the English secretary of state for Wales at the time of writing, echoing the centralized conservatism of the 'New Right', regards his charge as a region (when his former minister of state Sir Wyn Roberts has termed it a state, and John Major a nation). Yet he is only expressing

F.8   the same view as that held by Neil Kinnock in 1975 (F.8). Kinnock echoed Aneurin Bevan's famous attack on Welsh nationalism on 17 October 1944, denying that there was any marked difference between Wales's problems and those of any other industrial region. Yet even Kinnock has altered his position. 'Welshness' seems to mark significant and increasing party-political differences.

There are Welsh persons in the Conservative hierarchy — Michael Heseltine, Lord Howe, Michael Howard, Kenneth Baker, even (by descent) Lady Thatcher — but can we define them as such? Many are both 'British' and anti-European. Their only remaining Welsh clients have been those in the small-business sector, commuters, the population of the border districts and those who have retired to live along the northern littoral. Moreover, there is also an element which consciously seeks to mollify Welsh interest groups (and, perhaps, to divide and rule), as with Lord Walker's stint in the Welsh Office, 1987–90, during which time the partnership agreement with Baden-Württemberg was signed, and the more recent offer of enhanced representation in the Committee of the Regions, said to stem from John Major's 'special relationship' with Dafydd Wigley. The Welsh administrative state has continued to grow, even if the result — nationalism by quango — seems inherently unstable.

Labour's position arises from the three traditions which flow into the party. The early Independent Labour Party espoused much of the *gwerin* values of radical liberalism, including home rule, supported by Keir Hardie at Merthyr and James Griffiths at Llanelli. Proletarian internationalism regarded the miners as the vanguard of the class struggle, and some activists, such as Thomas Nicholas (Niclas y Glais) and S.O. Davies, aligned this with a radical communitarian sense. Others, notably Bevan, disapproved of a Welsh policy as reactionary, a view which

Aerial view of Cathays Park, Cardiff, showing the Welsh Office and the Temple of Peace, *c.*1960. (*Source: Welsh Industrial and Maritime Museum.*)

dominated in the 1950s and 1960s. The Communists in the NUM and other left-wing unions maintained their links with eastern Europe, although this meant increasingly 'going through the motions' of fealty to grossly imperfect 'workers' states'. Might matters have been different if a federal Spanish republic had won the civil war? Later, as heavy industry declined, the Labour movement took on a more nationalist position, not far from that of James Griffiths and Cledwyn Hughes. This middle-class neo-*gwerin* line ran into the débâcle of 1 March 1979, but since then, there has been a swing back to a more nationalist position. Yet Labour remains governed by its own priorities for attaining national power in the United Kingdom, in which the votes of Welsh MPs are essential. Outside the ranks of the Welsh MEPs and local authorities, how much interest is taken in European and international policy by the Welsh Labour movement?

The Liberals took longer to decline in Wales than elsewhere, as it proved difficult to budge the rural community from its Nonconformist radicalism. But they are now peculiarly weak in Wales in electoral terms, business supporters going to the right, and the *gwerin* ending up in Labour or Plaid Cymru. Yet they retain an élite following which remains important in national voluntary bodies and maintains elements of the old pacifist and internationalist tradition. Plaid Cymru, in many ways the origin-ators of the 'Wales in a Europe of the Regions' scenario, has moved from opposition to the European Community in the 1960s to enthusiasm. This was initially because the Common Agriculture Policy (CAP) regime benefited their rural farming constituency; more recently, because they, in common with all the other anti-Conservative parties, see the conflict between Westminster and Brussels as a means of constraining a Westminster rule which they find increasingly oppressive.

Manufacturing the Welsh State

Political parties exist first and foremost to represent interest groups. But where an administrative structure is erected, as with the Welsh Office in 1964, it will impose its own set of relationships. Effectively, the Welsh Office, created by and for James Griffiths, reflected both his 'Lib-Lab' *gwerin* outlook, and the equation that he made between Welsh self-government and the colonies which he sought to usher towards freedom while colonial secretary, 1950–1. But it had also to cope with the decline of the Welsh economy, which weakened the Conservatives as inheritors of Liberal industrialism in the 1920s, when its controllers were already migrating to London. (The *Dictionary of Business Biography* has few Welsh entries after about 1920.)

Labour's traditional base was the mining communities, the orphans of the 'Atlantic economy' of the Welsh heavy industries. But coal now fed the electricity-supply industry, and the networks of 'imperial Wales' — importing iron ore, copper and tin and pit-prop timber from Spain, America and the Baltic, and exporting steam-coal and anthracite world-wide — were abandoned. Steelmaking, likewise, concentrated on supplying strip to the West Midlands motor industry. Both industries were state-controlled after 1947–50. By the 1960s the 'Atlantic economy' was in a bad way, and with it many of the international connections that had been built up. What had come in its place?

In the 1960s the new 'Fordist' oil-and-car economy brought massive investment to Milford Haven, but few jobs. But, on the new industrial estates, the first German factories were opened in 1966; now there are fifty-five. There were only four Japanese employers in the whole of Britain in 1972, two of them in Wales; now Wales has the largest single agglomeration of Japanese-owned plants in Britain, if not in Europe. Add to this firms settling from other parts of Europe and America, warehouses for spare parts and the beginnings of research and development, and a new type of foreign representation is coming to maturity, which has arguably shifted Wales from the 'north' to the 'south' of the British economy (F.3).

F.3

The promotional and subsidy efforts of the Welsh Office and Welsh Development Agency are as 'international' as the diplomacy of sixty years ago. Multinational firms like Sony or Philips have, these days, turnovers as big as most members of the United Nations, and understanding their policy-formation and the motives that go into it is practically a subdivision of diplomacy. Are such firms footloose, motivated by low wage-rates and available public subsidies, prepared to move away to a new green-field site when a factory comes up for re-equipping? Are they drawn by the prospect of 'critical mass': the notion that once a particular level of development in one manufacturing area has been reached, the skills, economies of scale, infrastructure, will be of such high quality that other plants in the same line of business will be attracted? The longer-term outcome of this is that more high-value-added jobs will be attracted — in marketing, product development and systems control.

F.3   The result of research undertaken in Scotland's 'Silicone Glen' is not particularly reassuring about 'critical mass'. A lot of high-technology firms have been attracted, but only in their mass-production aspects (F.3). Management and high-value operations have stayed away, even in activities like offshore oil, although this may change as profit margins in the North Sea shrink and firms move to Aberdeen out of compulsion rather than choice. Another approach to attracting management is more pro-active: to boost facilities for such activities as conferences, in the hope that the good (and relatively cheap) facilities, communications and cultural provision on show will mean that firms will be induced either to settle more headquarters' operations in Wales, or to transfer to the country some of their annual training/social/promotional activities.

However, one might be less than sanguine following the saga of Wales's own design-led multinational Laura Ashley, lost in the 1980s to City of London speculators.

People to People

In Wales's case the post-industrial economy also involves the high-value-added end of tourism: what you could call the Swiss role. In this, an industry blurs its boundaries with society, or (less happily) with the 'life-style' of the advertising men. Which brings us to the international links created by the processes of socialization, which lie in family, community, education and religion.

These have shown many fractures. The Welsh family as working unit, threatened in the 1920s with redundancy, responded by
partial emigration, creating lateral links with the Welsh abroad,
and in London and the English Midlands, thus promoting integ-
ration and 'Britishness' — the burden of many novels by
Raymond Williams, who set out to 'measure the distance'
between 'community' and 'society', from *Border Country* (1961)
to *Loyalties* (1985). There was also a strong contrast between
transatlantic and European relationships. The former were
politically radical, but also had a strong historical and religious
continuity, whether with Welsh settlements in Pennsylvania or
Patagonia, or with other cosmopolitan-industrial immigrant
communities. The latter involved going back to older, pre-
Reformation links, of scholars and the Catholic Church. Thus
Saunders Lewis's idea of a self-governing, autarchic, de-industri-
alized Wales in a European Christendom was essentially an
anti-revolutionary, anti-Nonconformist, anti-Atlantic ideal,
F.9   based on Catholic social teaching (F.9).
Welsh education made foreign affinities complex. Old
Testament studies and prophetic books aligned many
Nonconformists with the Holy Land and quests for 'Beulah
Land'. This affiliation was generally undermined by secularization, but retains some almost alarming trace-elements: Ian
Paisley and Reinhard Bonnke, two highly political fundamental-
ists, influential respectively in Northern Ireland and Africa,
trained in Welsh Bible colleges. In Victorian Wales the public
education ideal was Janus-faced. It was orientated simultaneously towards the community and the state: an Arnoldian
compromise in which the 'nurturing' community was Welsh-
speaking while the 'achieving' state was English-speaking.
There was an attempt to get away from this in the radical wing
of Plaid Cymru and the advocacy by Drs D.J. and Noelle
Davies, of Scandinavian co-operation and of the educational
pattern of the Danish *Folkshogskolen*, so lessening the disciplin-
arian 'chapel' penumbra of language, temperance and religion
and leading to the more humane folk-culture of the Urdd
(1932) and of the Llangollen International Eisteddfod (1947).
This is one form of Welsh cultural internationalism. Another
— defining culture in its widest and least discriminating

Llangollen International Eisteddfod. *(Source: Wales Tourist Board.)*

sense — has been literally dramatic. Dylan Thomas, Emlyn Williams, Tom Jones, Shirley Bassey, Geraint Evans, Gwyneth Jones, Richard Burton and Anthony Hopkins have all essentially been performers. 'There are no Welsh actors because they are all in the pulpit,' Burton said, and this suggests a way in which the secularization of chapel culture has led on to an international stage — with the male-voice choir as much as with Dylan Thomas's poems. Culture establishes itself by tours and festivals, and these create their own international network of expectation and recognition. But the Welsh 'superstars' have also created a universal-and-local image (however fabricated) which strengthens the notion of a 'national' base.

Something similar affects literature. Its scope is necessarily more restricted, but the Welsh language is linked to an international network of scholars, and Welsh writing in English is also achieving greater recognition abroad. Figures such as Richard Hughes and R.S. Thomas address themes — environmental, psychological, political — which are recognized as universal as well as stemming from the Welsh experience. Ned Thomas, who encountered a particular political vocabulary, recognized the impact on Wales both of change in Europe and of the declining metropolitan centre (F.10). Both lay behind the foundation of the magazine *Planet* in 1971, with its strong subtitle 'The Welsh Internationalist', and its determination to remove parochialism from Wales: its vocabulary was aided by entry to Europe and by the regional conflicts in France and Spain, as well as by the increasing travails within the Soviet empire.

F.10

That *Planet* in its first flourishing (1971–9) coincided with the immediacy of an ecological crisis was also no coincidence. Environmental issues had high priority in Wales because the identification of language, tradition and nationalism encouraged resistance to the flooding of valleys for reservoirs and the indiscriminate planting of conifers, and because of such violent reminders of a distorted ecology as the Aberfan disaster in 1966. For all its reactionary sentimentalism, there was no escaping Richard Llewellyn's *How Green was my Valley* (1939). In turn, environmentalism went international with the involvement in Welsh affairs of 'small is beautiful' theorists such as Leopold Kohr, and the movement for alternative technology, centred at Machynlleth.

International sport generates more systematic relationships. It would be interesting to see how nations establish themselves in this way, but the pattern formed, say, by rugby must be influential, if eccentric. It takes in the 'five nations' but also South Africa and Romania — once embarrassing partners. But, unquestionably, success in it creates an international presence: New Zealand, with scarcely a million inhabitants in 1905, has demonstrated that! At the same time, British external representation in soccer and rugby reflects a pattern of organization dating from about twenty years before football was systematically structured in Europe. There were four UK nations in the World Cup pool, none of which qualified in 1994, and only one team from a united Germany: an ominous pointer? Nevertheless, the Welsh supporters with their red-and-white scarves and their singing have been a more welcome sight than some sports fans.

Then there are what A.J.P. Taylor called 'The Trouble Makers': the politicians and activists who take an active and awkward role in international affairs. Wales was not just a stamping ground for W.E. Gladstone and his great, if ambiguous theme, of 'international public right'; its earlier role in the formation of the Peace Society is obviously critical here, as is the Nonconformist commitment to pacifist principles which grew throughout the latter part of the nineteenth century. Henry Richard, by no means a supporter of home rule, would probably have agreed with Victor Hugo's address to the Paris Peace Conference in 1849, although on this occasion he met the French foreign minister, Alexis de Tocqueville, who was F.11 more of a regionalist (F.11). This commitment was reinforced later in the nineteenth century by the development of the Eisteddfodau and their pan-Celtic outlook, and by European interest in Welsh art and antiquity. However, pacifist enthusiasm may have been overestimated by Nonconformity, not noticeably anti-imperialist at the time of the Boer War, and its reputation was badly disrupted by the role of Lloyd George in swinging the country behind militancy in the First World War. Despite the efforts of Lord Davies of Llandinam in drumming up support for collective security, and creating the Temple of Peace and Health in Cardiff in 1938 — one may speculate what the commitment to the League of Nations Union would have looked like without him — neither Nonconformity nor Welsh pacifism was ever quite the same again.

Junctures

Up to now I have dealt with solid interests and tendencies, modified and deflected by individuals and campaigns, but broadly stable. These were stable because they represented social and economic forces; also because the politics of the Welsh state was not sufficiently virile to deflect them. But there was a significant multiple shift in Welsh attitudes involving the foregoing factors, and more, between about 1964 and the mid-1980s, when many of the old Anglo-Welsh bonds broke down. The creation of a secretary of state for Wales did not curb nationalism, although, after Gwynfor Evans had won Plaid Cymru's first seat in 1966, George Thomas was installed by Harold Wilson precisely for that purpose. What had more repercussions was the process of UK entry into the EEC, starting — as far as Wales was concerned — with a report of the re-formed Welsh Council in 1971. Entry was negotiated diplomatically by Edward Heath in 1973 and confirmed by the referendum of 1975. In 1975, Labour in Wales was even more fiercely opposed to entry into Europe than was Transport House — and their efforts were equally fruitless.

But where did Wales fit into Europe? In the 1970s a fashionable template among some socialists and nationalists was provided by the American sociologist Michael Hechter, whose paradigm of 'internal colonialism' saw the deliberate exploitation of the country under British rule, and hypothesized this continuing into a new European peripherality, in which Wales could be equated with the Basque country, Brittany and Corsica F.12 (F.12). This played a part in the intellectual and European politics of Welsh nationalism, but in the circumstances the theory of the Scots revisionist Marxist Tom Nairn was probably more influential. In an extended essay of 1973, Nairn saw European entry as a fatal blow to the dominant British-patriotic 'establishment' of Labourism, which had habitually dissolved both class

WALES GET BRITAIN OUT CAMPAIGN COMMITTEE

Safeguard your Job !

Safeguard your Freedom !

Safeguard your Future !

Safeguard your Children !

and

Strengthen Britain !

VOTE 'NO'

on June 5th

VOTE

YES

TO KEEP WALES IN EUROPE

"My advice to Wales is clear and unambiguous: To vote YES to stay in The Common Market"

Rt. Hon. JOHN MORRIS

Q.C., M.P. (Labour)

Secretary of State for Wales   22nd April, 1975

Issued by

WALES IN EUROPE

12 FREDERICK STREET, CARDIFF

Leaflets issued during the 1975 referendum about EEC membership. (*Source: a private collection.*)

and civic consciousness into Westminster's version of the
nation (F.13).

But it was notable that, after the country had voted for acces-
sion (in roughly the same proportion as the rest of the United
Kingdom), the appointed Welsh Labour MEPs rapidly moved
in a pro-Europe direction. Roy Jenkins was president of the
Commission in 1977–81 (although there are precious few references to Wales in his voluminous diaries) and a Welsh Labour
loyalist, Ivor Richard, became an EEC Commissioner in the
1980s (although his 'Wales and Europe' lecture of 1983 is no
more informative in this area). However, Plaid Cymru speedily
ditched its hostility and helped promote the Bureau of
Unrepresented Nations, founded in Brussels in 1975. These
connections survived even after the setbacks of 1979; and they
helped provide international networks which could be used by
Wales's new media after 1982. As European states became
more decentralized in the 1980s they, and their newspapers and
broadcast media, found it convenient to patronize autonomy
movements in the British Isles as a means of embarrassing Mrs
Thatcher, simultaneously (and illogically) arch-centralist and
dismantler of the British welfare state. The irony was that
Wales's alignment was more with the 'bourgeois regions' of the
European 'core' than with its traditional partners on the periphery (F.14).

Wales's European position was significant for three reasons.
First, being near to England was, for once, an advantage. Wales
was closer to Heathrow than some London suburbs on the
other side of the M25. Secondly, because it possessed an
administrative structure of its own, it was better placed to cooperate with other European regions than were English
regions, notably through its partnership agreement with Baden-
Württemberg in March 1990. Thirdly, as a land-bridge between
Europe and Ireland it had at least one potential ally on developmental matters. We might also add the language: a prevalent
bilingualism, or something near to it, did not seem to have done
the Swiss, Scandinavians or Catalans any harm.

Can we therefore think of Wales as well as Scotland taking a
special route to autonomy in Europe? Back to Lord Elis
Thomas, who sees this as more the cumulative effect of

F.13

F.14

F.6 administrative initiatives, political culture and policy patterns than the result of any concerted political campaign (F.6). The country's present pro-Europeanism seems to fit into two political tendencies: the drift of political power from the traditional defence-based nation-state to Brussels and to the regions, and the destruction of coercive multinationality in the former Soviet Union and its satellites.

Wales's current cosmopolitanism is genuine, but may also gloss over two things. The first is the international confrontation of rich and poor which Aneurin Bevan, a man who thought imaginatively about foreign policy, believed could be tackled by diverting arms accumulation into developmental F.15 measures (F.15). The role of the European region is not simply one of furthering its own development, but one of aiding the type of political development that Bevan was envisaging, through social and medical reform and intermediate technology. The second is the local breakdown to which Beatrix Campbell draws attention in her analysis of the 1991 riots in F.16 Ely, Cardiff, with their pronounced racial elements (F.16).

So it is worth thinking again about the Richard Hughes F.1 quotation (F.1) cited at the beginning of this essay. With 'post-industrialization' and the decline of the nation-state, who are now the 'we' and the 'they' in Welsh politics? Where are the dividing lines now going to occur? Where could the lava spurt on to the green Welsh grass?

Sources

F.1 . . . suppose that in the name of emergent reason the very we–they line itself within us had been deliberately so blurred and denied that the huge countervailing charges it once carried were themselves dissipated or suppressed? The normal penumbra of the self would then become a no-man's land: the whole self-conscious being has lost its footing . . . In such a state the solipsist *malgré-lui* may well turn to mad remedies, to pathological dreaming; for his struggles to regain his footing would indeed be an upheaval from being's very roots . . . gurgling up hot lava suddenly on to the green grass.

(Richard Hughes, *The Fox in the Attic*, Harmondsworth, Penguin, 1975, pp.99–100.)

F.2   In the long and varied list of subjects chosen for the classes conducted by the University in 1948–9 the lead was taken by the language, literature and history of Wales (66), well in front of international relations (42) and economics and political science (32). In 103 of the 356 classes the language used was Welsh.

(On the Dolgellau Eisteddfod) . . . And the effect was curious. I felt I was in a foreign country, friendly but foreign. It might have been the Bernese Oberland or Czechoslovakia in its happier days.

(Sir Reginald Coupland, *Welsh and Scottish Nationalism*, London, Collins, 1954, pp.341, 348.)

F.3   The importance of inward investment to the Welsh economy should not be underestimated. By 1992 there were over 400 foreign-owned manufacturing companies in Wales, employing 70,000 people or just under 30% of the manufacturing work-force (up from 17% in 1979). Furthermore, statistical evidence contradicts the image of the 'fly-by-night' foreign concern, with overseas companies boasting higher wage levels, higher levels of investment per employee, more advanced production facil-ities and higher levels of value added than their domestic counterpart. This is partly due to the attraction of higher quality inward investment . . . (by) Bosch, Toyota and British Avionics . . . Sony, who began production of televisions at their Bridgend plant in 1974 . . . have undertaken a number of major expan-sions since then, including a major research and development centre employing over 200 graduates . . .

The fact that there are territorial agencies or, in the case of the Welsh Office, a Ministry with full Cabinet status and a territ-orial remit that incorporates a wide range of functions, including that played by the Department of Trade and Industry in England, has meant that Wales has been somewhat more capable of influencing its own economic trajectory than it might otherwise have been. Certainly, these institutions are envied in comparable parts of Britain that do not possess them.

(Philip Cooke, Kevin Morgan and Adam Price, *The Welsh Renaissance: Inward Investment and Industrial Innovation*, Cardiff, Regional Industrial Research Centre for Advanced Studies, 1994, pp.13, 51.)

F.4   And as I was green and carefree, famous among the barns
       About the happy yard and singing as the farm was home,
           In the sun that is young once only,
               Time let me play and be
           Golden in the mercy of his means,
    And green and golden I was huntsman and herdsman, the calves
  Sang to my horn, the foxes on the hills barked clear and cold,
           And the sabbath rang slowly
          In the pebbles of the holy streams.

(Dylan Thomas, from 'Fern Hill', in *Collected Poems 1934–1952*, London, J.M. Dent, 1952, p.159.)

F.5   WALES

An independent pamphlet of creative work by the younger progressive Welsh writers.

British culture is a fact, but the English contribution to it is very small. MacDiarmid told the Scots that they could gain nothing by joining forces with the English and aping their mannerisms.

There is actually no such thing as 'English' culture: a few individuals may be highly cultivated, but the people as a whole are crass.

Welsh culture is carried on, not by a clique of moneyed dilettantes, but by the small shopkeeper, the blacksmith, the non-conformist minister, by the miners, quarrymen, and the railwaymen.

The Kelt's heritage is clear as sunlight, yet the burden of

English literature has also fallen on him. The greatest of present-day poets are Kelts.

We publish this journal in English so that it may spread far beyond the frontier of Wales, and because we realize the beauty of the English language better than the English themselves, who have so shamefully misused it.

We are beyond the bigotry of unintelligent fascist nationalism. In case the English should claim our contribution for their own, we produce this pamphlet, calling it 'Wales' in defiance of parasitic adoption.

Though we write in English, we are rooted in Wales.

(Keidrich Rhys, *Wales*, No. 1, Summer 1937.)

F.6 The most striking feature of the Welsh Office for Welsh media watchers is that it has become the most prominent place in Wales in which to protest. Demonstrations about everything from the government's policy in the Middle East and the Gulf War across to the closure of the smallest one-class primary school, not to mention health services, farming, chemical pollution, the poll tax, higher education cuts, all these conflicts about power and resources in and against the political system are acted out in front of that building. This is the actually existing government of Wales. It is the state of Wales. Secretaries of State for Wales, particularly the previous incumbent (Peter Walker), acted as if they were prime ministers of Wales. Flanked by motor-cycle outriders speeding out of Stuttgart Airport, on yet another European high tech trail. And what were these outriders there to protect him against?

(Dafydd Elis Thomas, Lord Nant Conwy, 'The Constitution of Wales', in Bernard Crick (ed.), *National Identities*, Oxford, Political Quarterly/Blackwell, 1991, p.65.)

F.7 Some kind of human society, though God knows what kind, will no doubt go on occupying these two western peninsulas of Britain, but that people, who are my people and no mean people, who have for a millennium and a half lived in them as Welsh people, are nothing but a naked people under an acid rain.

(Gwyn A. Williams, *When Was Wales?*, London, Black Raven Press, 1985, p.305.)

F.8   If I had to use a label of any kind, I should have to call myself a unionist. I believe that the emancipation of the class which I have come to this House to represent, unapologetically, can best be achieved in a single nation and in a single economic unit, by which I mean a unit where we can have a brotherhood of all nations and have the combined strength of working class people throughout the whole of the United Kingdom brought to bear against any bully, any Executive, any foreign power, any bureaucratic arrangement, be it in Brussels or in Washington, and any would-be colonialist, either an industrial colonialist or a political colonialist.

(Neil Kinnock MP, in *Hansard*, 3 February 1975, cited in John Osmond, 'Wales in the 1980s', in Charles R. Foster (ed.), *Nations without a State: Ethnic Minorities in Western Europe*, New York, Praeger, 1980, p.48.)

F.9   As Wales has been ruined from without, so it can only be restored from within . . . The entire natural resources of Wales are to be carefully developed in the interests of the Welsh people and to assist her neighbours in other parts of the world . . . It is the small successful countries of Europe, Sweden, Belgium, Denmark, Ireland, who stir our emulation, because they have all been faced with crises similar to ours, and have shown us by their example how such crises may be overcome.

(J.E. Daniel, *Welsh Nationalism: What it Stands for*, London, Foyle's Welsh Co., 1937, p.50 ff.)

F.10   I had grown up with the word extremist almost constantly in my newspaper — Kenya, Cyprus, Israel, Malaya, Aden; very often the word changed to terrorist and then one day the words would disappear and the head of a new independent state would arrive in London to meet the Queen.

(Ned Thomas, *The Welsh Extremist*, London, Victor Gollancz, 1971, p.1.)

F.11   A day will come when you, Russia — you, Italy — you, England — you, Germany — all of you, will, without losing your distinctive qualities and glorious individuality, be blended into a superior unity, and constitute a European fraternity, just as Normandy, Brittany, Burgundy and Lorraine have been blended into France.

(Henry Richard quoting Victor Hugo addressing the Paris International Peace Conference, 1849, cited in Goronwy J. Jones, *Wales and the Quest for Peace*, Cardiff, University of Wales Press, 1969, p.21.)

F.12   Commerce and trade among members of the periphery tend to be monopolised by members of the core. Credit is similarly monopolised. When commercial prospects emerge, bankers, managers and entrepreneurs tend to be recruited from the core. The peripheral economy is forced into complementary development to the core, and thus becomes dependent on external markets, when this economy rests on a single primary export, either agricultural or mineral. The movement of peripheral labour is determined solely by forces exogamous to the periphery. Typically there is great migration and mobility of peripheral workers in response to price fluctuations of exported primary products. Economic dependency is reinforced through judicial, political and military measures. There is relative lack of services, lower standards of living, and higher levels of frustration, measured by such indicators as alcoholism among members of the peripheral collectivity. There is national discrimination on the basis of language, religion, or, in general, ethnicity. Thus the structural differences between groups are causally linked to cultural differences.

(Michael Hechter, *Internal Colonialism*, London, Routledge, 1975, pp.33–4.)

F.13   Labourism stands not for class and nation — that is the ideological halo — but for class-in-nation; or more exactly, for nation-over-class. Labourism is (to employ one of its own historic programme-words in a different sense) the Nationalisation of class . . .

Labourism constitutes, perhaps, the most important element in the astonishing homogeneity of modern Britain. In effect, the most dangerous seam of civil society, the division between the classes, runs through it rather than outside it and is constantly 'healed' (that is, kept closed) by the very structure and world-view of the party . . .

The Labour Left almost never stands for class against nation, for the material reality of which Labourism is the mystical shell.

Were it so, the Labour Party could not exist in its actual form, and would certainly never have survived the trials of the past twenty years without a split.

(Tom Nairn, *The Left against Europe*, London, Pelican, 1973, pp.51–4.)

F.14   Within Europe, what makes for a politically assertive region? In the sixties and seventies there was a great deal of protest in areas that perceived themselves as poor, peripheral and colonised but which had a cultural movement — Wales, Brittany, Occitania (Spain offered a different context when minority nationalities asserted themselves explosively after the end of the Franco regime) . . .

But today in Western Europe, we see the rise of a different kind of regionalism. In Italy in the recent elections the good showing of the Lega Lombarda asserts a rich region's unwillingness to subsidise the poor south and the corrupt bureaucracy of Rome. The arguments are not dissimilar from those which fuelled the Slovene and Croatian critique of the old Yugoslavia — they wanted to join the richer West and have now succeeded in getting half way there.

(Ned Thomas, 'Post-Election Blues and Greens and Reds: Political Trends in the New Europe', *Planet*, No.93, June/July 1992, pp.5–6)

F.15   We are not in a situation where great empires are quarrelling about spoil and inheriting the corpses of those they have extinguished . . . The great powers of today, as they look at the armaments they have built up, find themselves hopelessly frustrated. If that be the case, what is the use of speaking about first, second and third class powers? That is surely the wrong language to use. It does not comply with contemporary reality. What we have to seek are new ways of being great, new modes of pioneering, new fashions of thought, new means of inspiring and igniting the minds of mankind. We can do so.

(Aneurin Bevan in the House of Commons, 19 December 1956, *Hansard,* Vol. 562, cols.1398–1407).)

F.16   What vexed all the 'authorities' was what to do about a crowd that thought it was simply claiming the right of congregation, the right to own its own space. The Rev. Robert Morgan remembered the atmosphere as being like 'a rave, a scene'. For all the sense of festivity, people were throwing bottles at Waheed's shop and singing 'Old MacDonald had a farm' at the police. It was also a crowd whose presence had a purpose — it wanted to torch a neighbour.

(Beatrix Campbell, *Goliath: Britain's Dangerous Places*, London, Methuen, 1993, p.21.)

Further Reading

Any comprehensive list of articles and books, even for such a relatively short period, would be prohibitively lengthy. It would embrace text-books, monographs, biographies, autobiographies, county histories and articles in a wide range of academic and more popular journals, without exploring the plethora of media material now available. This book already furnishes a wide range of references by means of the sources used in each chapter. For readers wishing to build up a comprehensive list there is a bibliography of Welsh history, compiled by Philip Henry Jones and updated to 1988. It is available in microfiche. The most comprehensive review of historical works appearing on Welsh history is provided by the *Welsh History Review*, published biennially by the University of Wales Press. This journal, along with *Llafur: The Journal of Welsh Labour History*, *Planet: The Welsh Internationalist* and *Contemporary Wales*, includes articles on specialist and general aspects of recent Welsh history.

The list which follows is, therefore, merely introductory, indeed it consists in the main of recently published general works on the history of Wales which have relevant chapters on the post-war period. A very few more specialist works have been included.

Jane Aaron, Teresa Rees, Sandra Betts and Moira Vincentelli (eds.), *Our Sisters' Land: The Changing Identities of Women in Wales*, Cardiff, 1994.

John Aitchison and Harold Carter, *A Geography of the Welsh Language 1961–1991*, Cardiff, 1994.

Tony Curtis (ed.), *Wales: The Imagined Nation. Essays in Cultural and National Identity*, Bridgend, 1986.

Janet Davies, *The Welsh Language*, Cardiff, 1993.

John Davies, *A History of Wales*, London, 1993 (published in Welsh as *Hanes Cymru*).

Christopher Harvie, *Europe and the Welsh Nation* (the Welsh Political Archive Lecture, 1984), Aberystwyth, 1995 (this pamphlet provides an extended treatment of the essay 'Wales and the Wider World').

Philip Jenkins, *A History of Modern Wales*, London, 1992.

Angela John, *Our Mothers' Land: Chapters in Welsh Women's History, 1830–1939*, Cardiff, 1991.

Gareth Elwyn Jones, *Modern Wales: A Concise History* (second edition), Cambridge, 1994.

Kenneth O. Morgan, *Rebirth of a Nation: Wales 1880–1980*, Cardiff/Oxford, 1981. (This book contains the most readily available comprehensive bibliography covering the period to 1980.)

John Osmond (ed.), *The National Question Again: Welsh Political Identity in the 1980s*, Llandysul, 1985.

Gareth Rees and Teresa Rees (eds.), *Poverty and Social Equality in Wales*, London, 1980.

Dai Smith, *Wales! Wales?*, London, 1984.

Meic Stephens, *The Arts in Wales: 1950–1975*, Cardiff, 1979.

M. Wynn Thomas, *Internal Difference: Literature in Twentieth-Century Wales*, Cardiff, 1992.

Ned Thomas, *The Welsh Extremist*, London, 1971; (second edition, 1991, contains 'The Welsh Extremist Revisited — a Postscript in 1990', originally published in *Planet*).

David Williams and Ieuan Gwynedd Jones, *A History of Modern Wales* (second edition), London, 1977.

Gwyn A. Williams, *When Was Wales?*, London, 1985.

Index

Page references in *italics* refer to Illustrations